Spiritual and Physical Health

By

CHARLES S. PRICE

Price

CHARLES S. PRICE PUBLISHING COMPANY, INC.
2100 Brigden Road
Pasadena 7, California

*A non-profit corporation organized for the purpose of spreading
the truths of the Gospel of Jesus Christ throughout the earth.*

CONTENTS

CHAPTER I

IT SHALL BE DONE

"But without faith it is impossible to please Him: for he that cometh to God must believe that He IS, and that He is a RE-WARDER of them that diligently seek Him." (Heb. 11:6)

IF WE ARE seeking healing for the body, we will seek to PLEASE GOD, and the Scripture says that without faith it is impossible to please Him. But we cannot have this faith unless we experience the joy of His indwelling presence, for it is something more than an intellectual belief in God. It is the FAITH OF GOD; the faith which He imparts; the faith which radiates from His indwelling. It is the Son in us that pleases the Father. So many suffering ones focus their attention on the pain which they are suffering, rather than on their SOURCE of supply, and in so doing they hinder the healing flow of God.

Our need in time of sickness and suffering may

seem to be very real and, indeed, it is. But it is no more real than the eternal fact of His illimitable supply! "But my God shall supply ALL YOUR NEED according to His riches in glory by Christ Jesus." (Phil. 4:19) It is not in dealing with our sickness and our symptoms that we find the deliverance for which we hunger, but it is the recognition of the riches of His grace and the consciousness of His inexhaustible supply!

Our God has made the promise, *"Behold I make all things new!"* He will PERFECT that concerning us and "to perfect" means to bring it up to God's standard and that standard is being COMPLETE IN CHRIST. Nothing less than that will do. It does not mean perfection in one's self; but perfection in Christ. A sinful man, in himself, can never develop the nature of a Holy God. We do not become so pure and holy in self that we develop the Divine Nature! It is rather that the grace of the Lord Jesus has made it possible for Him to come to the least and the weakest of us and, if we are willing, we can become PARTAKERS of the Divine Nature! He gives it! He imparts it! It overflows our spirit; it saturates our personality; it goes over our lives like a mighty flood! So we should not look at ourselves nor our sicknesses but rather look at Him, His Health and His Virtue! Remember again the far-reaching extent of His promise, "My God shall supply all your need according to His riches in glory by Christ Jesus!" That is the standard by which every need of spirit, soul and body is supplied. There is no reservation there. There is no withholding. We do not have a need of body, soul or spirit but what that promise covers it and He who has so wonderfully promised is able to fulfill His promise in our obedient, surrendered lives!

There are those people who have BELIEVED GOD, although they have not seen Him, but have had *entre* through Jesus Christ. They have come up through the Door which the Saviour is. They have experienced that healing flow that He pours forth into the body of His believers. These believing ones have not waited for that time of seeing the awakening "in His likeness" but, *in the present, they have believed God!* "Whom having not seen we love! In whom though now ye see Him not, yet believing, ye rejoice with joy unspeakable and full of glory!" (I Pet. 1:8) These victorious spirits have pressed through the maze of this world's affairs and the confusion of the flesh, until they are continually receiving that energizing, quickening power of God for spirit, soul and body! They are finding the Lord MORE THAN SUFFICIENT for every need of life. His presence permeates into every department of the entity which they are, and they not only experience the cleansing flow of Calvary, but their physical bodies are bathed in the gentle rays of the Divine Health which radiate from His indwelling like rays of the morning sun!

GOD IS FAITHFUL

The body may be continually attacked through the manifold results of the Fall, but God has promised to MAKE A WAY WHERE THERE IS NO WAY! "There hath no temptation (testing) taken you but such as is common to man, but GOD IS FAITHFUL, who will not suffer you to be tempted above that ye are able, but will with the temptation, also make a WAY TO ESCAPE, that ye may be able to bear it." (I Cor. 10:13) Let those words ring within your heart! HE IS FAITHFUL! HE IS FAITHFUL! He who has promised a way of escape will also provide that way of escape. We cannot manufacture it! He provides it and, in faith, we utilize that Divine provision. Faith laughs at impossibilities, and cries from the reality of knowing Him, *"It shall be done!"* O, glorious oneness with the triune God! What blessing we receive, when having not seen, WE HAVE BELIEVED! And, believing, we press through symptoms, trials, pains and perplexities! Not because of any virtue from our self, but because we have believed Him! When we believe HIM, we have no confidence in the flesh. The more we behold His glorious ability, the more we are convinced of our inability! We cannot; but He can! No longer do we lean on self, but we LEAN ON HIM! No matter how dark the night, the redeemed spirit sings, "He is able!" No matter how intense the suffering, we know that He is able! No matter how great the perplexity, we are assured that HE IS ABLE! We sing it triumphantly, victoriously, because we can do no other when we are conscious of His presence! Can darkness stand in the presence of the Light? When He is near, we are convinced that He is able to keep that which we have committed unto Him against that day. "For I know whom I have believed and am persuaded that He is able to keep that which I have committed unto Him against that day." (II Tim. 1:12) Sing in triumph through every adversity, perplexity and pain, "He is able," and we who love Him are so persuaded!

How enlightening are the words that Jesus spoke to the sufferers when He was here among men! "Believest thou that I am able to do these things?" Our exultant spirits cry, "Yes, Lord, Thou art able! Thou, and Thou alone!" Believest, thou, beloved, that these words are LIVING AND VITAL? Believest thou that GOD *IS* and that He is a REWARDER of them that diligently seek Him? It is not the reward that we receive at the end of this age. It is not waiting until some heaven opens up its gates to receive us. It is not in some far distant future to which we look through the windows of the promise, but it is HERE AND NOW! It is TODAY! God is not only the God of our tomorrows; He is the God of our todays. He DAILY loadeth us with benefits! "Blessed be the Lord who daily loadeth us with benefits, even the God of our Salvation!" (Ps. 68:19) He is the RE-WARDER of them that diligently seek Him! And the reward is not reserved for the future alone; it is imparted and infused here and now. *Today,* if you will hear His voice, harden not your hearts! *Today,* we should listen to the Divine pleading and give heed to the Divine call! Not as the fathers did when they hardened their hearts and refused to listen to the Voice that was calling them; but wandered around in an unnecessary wilderness for forty years! O, what grief we unnecessarily carry! O, what loads we bear! All because we do not realize that the things that we have been anticipating in our tomorrows, God, in His love and grace and mercy would impart to us today. Not only in the future, but in the here and now are we ACCEPTED IN THE BELOVED and that acceptance embraces every needy part of us: body, soul and spirit.

FULNESS OF JOY

David in Psalm 16:8-11 says: "I have set the Lord always before me: because He is at my right hand, I shall not be moved. Therefore my heart is glad, and my glory rejoiceth; my flesh also shall rest in hope. For thou wilt not leave my soul in hell; neither wilt thou suffer thine Holy One to see corruption. Thou wilt show me the path of life: in Thy presence is fulness of joy; at Thy right hand there *are* pleasures for evermore." There *are;* not will be. This is the victory that overcometh the world, even our FAITH! How wonderfully does the Spirit reveal the far reaching significance of those words: "Thou wilt not leave my soul in hell; neither wilt thou suffer thine Holy One to see corruption." As Christ was raised up by the quickening power of God and continually manifested to the incredulous world the glory and power and virtue invested in Him by the Father, so He is pleading with us, to DRAW NIGH, with full assurance, counting all things but loss that we might WIN CHRIST! "Let us draw near with a true heart, in full assurance of faith, having our hearts sprinkled from an evil conscience and our bodies washed with pure water!" (Heb. 10:22)

In days of old the Master stood with outstretched arms and broken heart, crying to the people of Jerusalem who insisted upon going about their own, preconceived ways and following out their daily pursuits. They were burdened and they were heavy laden; they were sorrowful and sinful and sick in body and soul. They must have looked to Him like the majority of people in this war-torn, weary world look, on the streets of every city in which dwell men! From the depths of His innermost being, He cried, "Come unto Me and I will give you rest!" That was the condition—that they come to Him! They were to find that rest in Him! How often would He have gathered them to Him, but they would not. He wanted them to abide under the shadow of the Almighty. He wanted to take their

broken bodies and give them His strength and His
healing. He wanted to take their sins and give them
His salvation. He wanted to take their impurities
and give them His holiness. He wanted to be ALL
to them that they needed and He would have been,
had they only listened to His plea and accepted His
invitation of grace. He knew that all of them would
be accepted by the Father in Him! But still they
went their own willful and sinful ways! The way to
God is THROUGH CHRIST and the way to Christ
is through FAITH; and the way to faith is through
SURRENDER of our will to God's will. We draw
near to God through the Blood of the Everlasting
Covenant. "Draw nigh to God and He will draw
nigh to you!" (James 4:8)

COMMITTING

We must not stumble because the answer does
not always come our way. "Commit thy way unto
the Lord; trust also in Him, and He shall bring it to
pass." Though sometimes He causes us to tarry for
a little while, it is always for our good. It is for the
development of those things in us that will cause us
to draw near and closer to His precious, wounded
side. He knows our frame; He understands our human frailities. He is fully conscious of the pain we
bear, and the suffering we endure. He knows; for
HE BORE IT IN HIS OWN BODY TO THE
TREE! It pleases Him, when in spite of symptoms

we trust Him, and in spite of the fact that the way may be, temporarily, dark, we have confidence that the light will shine through. The skies will be riven; the dark clouds will part asunder. God will vindicate His Word! The Son will manifest the answer to our prayers and work in us the fulfillment of His own promises. "Cast not away therefore your confidence, which hath GREAT RECOMPENCE OF REWARD. For ye have need of PATIENCE, that, after ye have done the will of God, ye might receive the promise. For yet a little while, and he that shall come will come, and will not tarry. Now the JUST SHALL LIVE BY FAITH; but if any man draw back, my soul shall have no pleasure in him. But we are not of them who draw back unto perdition; but of them that believe to the saving of the soul." (Heb. 10:35-39)

In Isaiah 42:3, we read, "A bruised reed shall He not break and the smoking flax shall He not quench; He shall bring forth judgment unto truth." So, if perchance, you find yourself filled with the glory of God, and you are made to feel the nearness of His Divine presence, thank Him! Praise Him! Treasure it as the most priceless gift that time affords us to know. If, perchance, you have followed afar off, thank God that at least your eyes have desired to see Him. If, indeed, there is only a trickle of faith—a cloud the size of a man's hand only, and that a distance away—thank God! Praise Him for that! The man and his servant who climbed up the steeps of Carmel knew what the promises were. In spite of the antagonism of a king and his entire country, THEY BELIEVED GOD! In spite of the unbelief of the entrenched ecclesiastical system, THEY BELIEVED GOD! It meant something for Elijah to believe God in that day! Believing God not only brought the fire that consumed the sacrifice, but it later brought the rain that ended the long period of famine and made the desert rejoice and blossom as a rose! After Heaven had answered the cry of the prophet on the summit of Carmel, there was still no sign of rain! But Elijah believed God!

Oh, what victories are won when men BELIEVE GOD! They do not believe the cloudless skies; they believe God! They do not believe the symptoms which exist and the conditions which surround them. They believe God! So, over and over again, Elijah's servant went out to the end of the promontory and looked out over the sea. Then it came! Only the size of a man's hand, but later it filled all the skies and the drenching rain came! The God of Heaven had answered and He is the One who never fails! So if you see the cloud the size of a man's hand, thank God for that and do not upbraid yourself or Him because the rain clouds do not instantly appear.

> *"Saw ye not the cloud arise,*
> *Little as a human hand?*

Now it spreads o'er all the skies,
Hangs o'er all the thirsty land.
Lo, the promise of a shower
Drops already from above,
But the Lord will shortly pour
All the fullness of His love."

He has prescribed for this very hour for you and for me! Keep on looking up, beloved! Look up above the degree of *your* faith— up above the thorns and the thistles—yes, look up, and be not afraid! The clouds are parting! The skies are being rent asunder! What He has promised He will also perform! He will not fail! Through the rift in the dark, we shall see in the vision that meets our gaze, something of the King in all His virtue and His beauty! Something of His radiant presence that has been flowing from the Throne ever since Time was! Something that will make our hearts pant after more of His flowing grace, even as the hart panteth after the waterbrooks! Even so will our souls and our spirits long and yearn for the Eternal God!

FOUR THINGS

There are four things our Father would have us remember. First, HE CALLETH FOR THEE! As in the days of Martha and Mary and the sorrow filled home at little Bethany, Jesus came in all the power of His lovely presence to lift them out of their despondency and to dry their eyes and wipe their tears

away! It was after she had met Jesus face to face
that Martha sought out her sister and said, "The
Master is come and calleth for thee!" That is the
message we would give you now. The Master is come
—and calleth for *thee!*

Secondly, HIS LOVE IS UPON THEE! In spite
of your weakness; yea, even transgression, His love
is upon thee! No matter how deep the night through
which you are passing, His love still overshadows
and His heart still yearns! His love is unfailing and,
like His very nature, knows no end! How the burdens lift when we begin to realize that HE LOVES
US! It is because of that Love Divine, all loves excelling, that we are permitted to drink of the fountains of His eternal supply just as He gave the woman
to drink by Samaria's wayside well!

Thirdly, HIS POWER IS FLOWING OUT
AND INTO THEE! Take it! Drink it! You cannot
drain such an ocean dry! It is not by might nor by
power, but by My Spirit, saith the Lord. When we
have tried the last vestige of human power—when
we have utilized the best and the greatest of human
might, be it of body or of brain, we come to the end
of self, and realize our own helplessness! Then the
river flows from beneath the Throne! Then the
waters of redeeming love and of His unfathomable
Spirit begin to flow. First, to the ankles; then to the
knees; then to the loins and, behold, ere long, we
have WATERS TO SWIM IN! Drink! Drink!

Drink! For you can never drain that river dry!

And, four, HE IS SUFFICIENT FOR THEE! One of old asked the question, "Who is sufficient for these things?" There is only one answer. He is! More than sufficient! We must not upbraid ourselves because of our lack of sufficiency. We must not fasten our eyes upon our shortcomings, but we must gaze upon the One who has been lifted up! He alone is sufficient! There was not life for a life-time of service. There was LIFE FOR A LOOK! There is life and health and strength and healing at this moment for thee! He *is* sufficient. He—and He alone.

I AM

When in the days of old, He came walking in the middle of the night toward His affrighted disciples, utilizing the side-walks of the sea, they were filled with fear! They thought they had seen a spirit. He was doing as He always does, a new and unusual thing. The night could not hold Him back. The storm could not detain Him. They needed Him and to them He must needs go. At the moment of their crying out in fear, His voice sounded over the waves, "I am! Be not afraid!" (Gr.) "*I am!*" He still is the great I AM! We must not say He *was* then— or He *is* now — or He *will be* in the future. We cannot separate Him from time, for He ALWAYS IS! He is still *I am!* He is approaching your boat. He is coming to you, walking upon the sea! He has

heard your cry and He does not upbraid. He knows
your fears, but He does not condemn. Rather does
He speak with that wonderful voice of assurance,
and fear cannot live when Jesus speaks His message
of assurance to your heart. Hearken, for He is speaking now within! "It is I—I am!—Be not afraid!"

So, beloved, draw nigh with full assurance! As
we turn toward God, our eyes shall behold Him with
outstretched arms toward us. We shall see Him
coming, walking to us upon the sea! Oh, turn ye—
turn ye—for why will ye die? Why will ye lack
when all things are provided, for spirit, soul and
body? He who loves us and gave Himself for us,
not only gave Himself for us then, but is giving
Himself to us now! Take Him! Receive Him! Drink
Him! Eat Him! Blessed Eternal Bread of Life!
Drink Him! Fountains of Living Water! Rivers
of Redeeming Grace! Behold Him! Praise Him and
love Him, for He is all you need.

CHAPTER II

THE NEW CREATION LIFE

THE FACT that God has help for *every* need of human life is apparent both in the written and the revealed Word. The glorious declaration of Divine truth from Genesis to Revelation is the story of the sufficiency of our God! In not a single instance, do we find any record of His insufficiency; and for body, soul and spirit He was the ETERNAL EL SHADDAI! *The God who was enough!*

To Him both men and nations turned when they had reached the final limits of the extremity of their own endeavors; and Law and Grace both revealed that He whose mercy endureth forever was the complete and perfect Redemption! The Curse was not bigger than the CURE! The Fall was not greater than the lifting power of the Lord! The Book which begins with the majesty of Creation, ends with the glory of Re-creation; and between the Alpha and the Omega, we behold the *saving, healing rays of our Heavenly Father!*

God is sufficient for everything. Absolutely everything! No matter in what realm we put it, the heavens are telling the story of His all-sufficiency. Is there anything too hard for God? Why then, are so many of God's dear children in need, both in body and soul, in spite of the vast reaches of His grace, and the magnitude of His redemption. More than healing—we need the Healer. More than deliverance we need the Deliverer. Why ask Him to give us "things" when He is everything we need. *He must increase as we decrease,* for we cannot see *God as He is,* unless we see ourselves as *we really are!* No man can see God and live. It will be death to the old nature. He is the INFUSER and the IMPARTER of the New Creation Life and this life will permeate body, soul and spirit and He will work in us the glorious miracle of transformation.

No matter how great *your need,* God is sufficient! No matter how dark the path may be, in the midst of bewildering and perplexing situations, His lovely presence will bring that light that will dispel the darkness and lead you into the liberty of that truth which always sets men free. Free from the law of sin and death! Free from the terrors of self-condemnation and free from the entanglements of our misunderstandings and misinterpretations! Free from the bonds which have held us back from walking out of our pain and diseases into the privileges of His radiant health! For have we not limited the measurements of the Atonement to boundaries which our human traditions and misinterpretations have erected instead of realizing that when Jesus shed His precious Blood on the Cross of Calvary and cried, "IT IS FINISHED," He meant exactly what He said. It *was* finished! The Atonement was consummated! Complete! And there was finality in the throbbing statement which came from the lips of our suffering Lord. He was wounded for our transgressions. He was bruised for our iniquities. The chastisement of our peace was upon Him, and with His stripes we are healed! The debt of sin has been paid. We have been taught with truth, of course, that He died to pay the debt of our iniquity. He gave His life and shed His blood upon the Cross to save us from our sins.

OUR INHERITANCE

But that was only *part* of the glorious inheritance! We died with Him that He might impart to us HIS LIFE. Not by works, lest any man should boast, but by the infinite alchemy of Grace, our very bodies, through Calvary were made temples and tabernacles of the Living God! He came that we might have LIFE, and that we might have it more abundantly! Not our lives; but His! We were offered the privilege of becoming so permeated with the gift of God which is Eternal Life through Jesus Christ our Lord, that we, in this present world, could become PARTAKERS OF THE DIVINE

NATURE! We were not told to *earn* the riches
which He purchased for us on the Cross of Calvary,
but rather were we to receive the fullness of our
inheritance, which is the indwelling of the Lord Jesus
Christ Himself!

A broken, bleeding world around us is crying
for DELIVERANCE! Little does it dream of the
way in which that deliverance will come. With what
clarity does the written Word speak of these transi-
tion days in which we live! They were to be days
of the REVELATION! They were to be days of the
OPENING OF THE UNDERSTANDING! They
were to be days of COMMUNION WITH GOD,
when mysteries would be revealed and light from the
hills shine upon things which have been cloaked in
partial obscurity. God is unfolding and revealing
Himself and His Eternal Truth, as we walk with
the Spirit along the paths of an unfolding Revelation!

The purpose of this book is to bring to view that
which God is making manifest. The truths which we
have received as doctrines must become transfigured
until they are flaming, vital realities that burn within
the spirit. In these tremendous days, it is not enough
"to know about it." We must *experience it—possess
it*—until the thing which once was a theology has
become so spiritually assimilated that it is part of our
very natures. The Living Christ Who has been viewed
merely historically by so many, must be formed with-

in us and the "Kingdom without" must be changed to the "Kingdom *within.*"

We have gazed back at the historic fact of Calvary somewhat sentimentally, and many have struggled to assent in their minds to the fact that He died there to save us from our sins. Then has come the attempt to try to live the Christian life. A struggle which has ended in disappointment and disillusionment and, sometimes, despair. We limited mortals can never live His life. So the love of our Father provided that He live His life in us. "My little children, of whom I travail in birth again, *until Christ be formed in you . . .*" (Galatians 4:19) is the text which opens the door to our complete emancipation and to health of spirit, soul and body! This is the eternal purpose which He purposed in Christ Jesus our Lord. The Spirit has been speaking to my heart! His truth has been burning within me! I feel like saying, "Paul, I know what you were talking about when you wrote, 'For this reason, on bended knee I beseech the Father, from whom the whole family in heaven and on earth derives its name, to grant you— in accordance with the wealth of His glorious perfections—to be strengthened by His Spirit with power permeating your inmost being. I pray that Christ may make His home in your hearts through your faith; so that having your roots deep and your foundations strong in love, you may become mighty to grasp the idea, as it is grasped by all the saints, of

the breadth and length, the height and depth—yes,
to know the love of Christ that surpasses knowledge,
so that you may be filled with all the fulness of God.
Now to Him who, in the exercise of His power THAT
IS AT WORK WITHIN US, is able to do infinitely beyond all our highest prayers or thoughts—to Him be
glory in the Church and in Christ Jesus to all gen-
erations, world without end!' " (Ephesians 3:14-21)
Weymouth.

THE LIFE LINE

That is the life-line which the poor, weary, tired
body can grasp! It is not a death line—but a life line.
That is the deliverance for the one who is almost
sinking in the turbulent seas of circumstance or
environment! Paul does not declare that *we* are able
to do it but that *He* is. It is not our power in Him;
it is His power in us. "Now to him who in the exercise of HIS POWER that is at work within us, is
able to do infinitely beyond all our highest prayers or
thoughts." That is why in a large sense, we should
not seek "Salvation," we should receive the SAV-
IOUR! Is Salvation something He imparts separ-
ately from Himself? He does not *give* Salvation—
HE IS IT. We should not try to attain "Healing"
and repeat, with heathen-like repetition, "I am
healed. I am healed. I am healed." But we should,
rather, allow the FLOW of His life from within. His
life! His power that is at work and in operation
within us will bring about the miracle which is be-

yond "all our highest prayers or thoughts." This is the wisdom which is born from above. This is the knowledge which is the experience of the *heart* and not of the *mind*. This is the revelation that surpasses the light of the noon-day sun! Paul declared, "It is the stewardship of the truth, which from all the ages lay concealed in the mind of God, the Creator of all things in order that the Church might now be used to display to the powers and authorities in the heavenly realms the innumerable aspects of God's wisdom." (Ephesians 3:9, 10)—*Weymouth*.

BECOMING

When Paul was stricken on the Damascus Road He did not say "What is this"? but "WHO ART THOU?" There is an infinity of difference between the two. Jesus did not try to change Saul's mind— He rather indwelt Him until Saul became Paul and he could declare of a truth, "For ME to live is CHRIST." He gives to all of us the "POWER TO BECOME!" Then when the surrender is made, He supplies the power by which we become! It is more than *believing*. It is *becoming*. It is far more wonderful than *doing*. It is *being*. And that makes it so easy instead of so hard! Instead of struggling to attain, we ALLOW HIM TO BE! As I look back over the ministry of praying for the sick, I can see now in the picture at the distance what I could not see when I was too close to the canvas, and the event. How

wonderful it is of my Lord to reveal these riches of
the inheritance of the saints to me in these later years!
How many times, I struggled and labored and prayed
and wept, only to come, in exhaustion, to the end of
my own endeavors. And how well I remember how
oft He came. Just as He came down the mountain-
side from the glory of the Transfiguration to where
the boy needed healing in the vales below! Like the
disciples, I had given my all, but my all was not
enough. *Jesus came!* He spoke! There was no effort;
no struggle; no battle. It was as though He exhaled
His very life into sick bodies and disease and pain
simply vanished!

He is still calling to us over the noise and the
tumult of our life's wild, restless sea! The storm may
have screamed at Him, but He did not scream at the
storm! There was more power in His peace than
there was in the fury of the tempest. There is more
dynamic in His love than there is in the cruelty of
suffering and of pain. When light comes into the
room, it does not struggle and battle and fight with
the darkness. It bursts forth with the radiance of
its illuminating power and the darkness is no more.
Thus it is with the Light of the world. He does not
give light. He is Light! Of what or whom can we
be afraid when the Lord is the Light of our lives?

How we humans have struggled with death! We
have fought with the enemy of our souls and have
we ever won the conflict except through Christ?

When the Resurrection and the Life stood in front of the tomb of Lazarus, He did not speak to death. He ignored it. The truth is that death was powerless; absolutely powerless, in the presence of the Resurrection and the Life. And Resurrection was not something He could *do*; neither was Eternal Life something which had been presented to Him. He *was* the Resurrection! He *was* Eternal Life. He was then, and He *is* now! So in His presence, death did not have authority and power. He did not rebuke it. He did not tell it to go away. He simply spoke to Lazarus and told him to come out of the grave. And when JESUS SPOKE, the Christ life in Lazarus was manifest.

ONLY JESUS

Is it not time that we, too, stepped out of the way, and allowed Him to do what, after all, He alone can accomplish? Only yesterday, a poor sufferer, honest and sincere before her Lord, came for prayer and to talk with us about healing and the things of God. Poor soul! How she had struggled! How like thousands of others of God's dear children, she had "done this" and "done that" and tried this and tried that until, in her own words, "I've almost come to the place of despair!" "Brother Price," she said, "what can I do? Tell me, and whatever it is, I will do it!" I think she was rather amazed at my answer. "My dear sister, perhaps your Lord is wanting to bring you to the place WHERE YOU DO NOTHING!

As I sit and talk to you about His love and grace in
the midst of your tremendous need, I cannot think
of anything YOU CAN DO in the light of the revelation
of what HE HAS DONE." I shall long remember the
light that came into her face as she laid her burden
down. Neither shall I soon forget the marvel of the
manifestation of His life as she went away!

How many times have we talked of miracles and
healing entirely in the *past tense*. We refer to the days
"when He was here," and have affirmed that the
glory of the Lord was manifest because in "those
olden days" the cities were blessed by His lovely
presence! That may be truth; but it is only part of
it. Everything within me cries out the declaration
that He is just as much here now as He was then!
There is a sense in which He is MORE here now
than He was then. In those days, if He were in Cana,
He was not in Judea. If He were on the mountain
alone with His Father, His disciples sought for Him
on the other side of the sea! He knew then the lim-
itation of a human body, for He came to us in the
form of a Man. But, today, He is the King of the
Kingdom within. If He is in Judea, He is also in
Galilee. If He is in the East, He is also in the West!
He dwells within the hearts of all who will receive
Him. RECEIVE HIM! Not acquiesce to dogma,
nor give intellectual assent to doctrine. RECEIVE
HIM! And to as many as will so do, He will give
the power to become sons, and what that SONSHIP

will, ultimately, lead to will some day stagger the world and set the angels to singing again the Story of the glory of the Lord!

CHAPTER III

RELEASED

THE BETTER we know Jesus the more we are convinced of the magnitude of His Redemption! We have done nothing to deserve it, and we  can do nothing to repay Him for it. It was born in Love, cradled in **Mercy and** imparted i n **Grace.** It c o v e r s BODY, SOUL AND SPIRIT! It touches every part of man. It permeates his will. It transforms his nature. It converts his disposition. So wonderful is it in its operation that not in doctrine, but in actuality, we are made new creations in Christ Jesus! The old things have passed away, and, behold, all things become new. The transforming, healing touch of the Holy Spirit will not only diffuse Himself through our spirits, but even our MORTAL BODIES are permeated with the healing rays of the Sun of righteous-

ness and disease and pain are banished like the darkness flees before the rising of the morning sun!

"And if the Spirit of Him who raised up Jesus
from the dead is dwelling in you, He who raised up
Christ from the dead will *give life also* to your
mortal bodies through His Spirit dwelling in you."
(Romans 8:11)—*Weymouth*. This is the Divine Key
which unlocks to us the doors that lead to our complete and perfect healing. Healing not only of body,
but of spirit and of soul! When we want to bring
light into a room, we do not try to cast the darkness
out, but we put the light in. It is vain to struggle to
get rid of our pains and our sufferings and even our
sins and our weaknesses. The only way one can rid
himself of the power of the devil is to admit and give
authority to the power of the Lord Jesus. We cannot
do it but HE CAN! No man can save himself by
abstinence from things which are sinful. That is why
salvation is not what we do, but what *we are*. We are
transformed into His image and, beholding that
Image, as in a glass, we are changed from glory to
glory, until at last we shall awaken completely IN
HIS LIKENESS! That is why whenever we hear
some of God's sincere, but immature children, pound-
ing away on the externals, we know that the glorious
light of the revelation of the truth as it is in
our blessed Lord has not yet fully come to them.
When we become LIKE HIM, we are delivered from
the bondage of the *outer*. Of course, that will reflect

the transformation in the inner. Then we abstain, not to *be* saved, but because we *are* redeemed.

The same is true when it comes to the healing of the body. In the days of old, virtue flowed from Jesus, when people pressed forward to touch Him. That virtue was an integral part of the Christ Himself. The disease simply could not abide in the presence of the Virtue! Can corruption continue when Incorruption takes the throne? Will mortality still exist when Immortality reigns? Have we not known that there is a law—a Divinely appointed and imparted law—and it is called THE LAW OF THE SPIRIT OF LIFE IN CHRIST JESUS! *It makes us free from the law of sin and of death!* It supersedes it. It overwhelms it. It makes it incapable of operation. Why should we try to remove by our own struggles the law of sin and death when such victory can only be brought about by the operation of the LAW OF LIFE in Him? In the last analysis, the goal of every mature Christian should not be Divine Healing but DIVINE HEALTH! The flow of His life through ours; the surrender of our will to His; the impartation of His nature, until our natures are impregnated with the glory and the presence of the Divine! Not in an instant! Not in some emotional moment at an altar! But by that daily acknowledgement of His lovely presence in ALL OUR WAYS, and the surrender of EACH MOMENT to His care and to His keeping.

THE RELEASE

There must come the RELEASE OF ONE'S SELF completely and entirely to God! When one's spirit, soul and body is truly KEPT FOR GOD, one can then say, of a truth that he is KEPT BY GOD! Until that comes, it is like running a high-powered car with the BRAKES ON! *Self* is the greatest deterrent to progress we know!

We say, "I gave myself to God—back there when I was saved—or during some moment of consecration." The revelation of His saving grace may have been instantaneous, but growth in that grace is, certainly, PROGRESSIVE. It is just like the growth of a child, for the analogy is used throughout the Word, and we should continue to grow until we come to the PERFECT MAN, to the fullness of the stature of Christ! It is as though one were given an automobile, say, at the time of Conversion. Then a little later, at the time of the Baptism in the Spirit, oil was given in order that the car would be able to run! Now we are out on the HIGHWAY, with "power to become"—to become sons of God! We may have received the power to become—and yet, NOT become! There has been no doubt about the gift of His Salvation. We might be in the car all right, but when *self* manifests itself, it acts as a BRAKE and a deterrent for our onward progress and our growth. We do not carry the car, but the car carries us. We must learn to RELEASE OURSELVES UNTO GOD! "It

is not by might nor by power but BY MY SPIRIT,"
saith the Lord. When we are in the Spirit we are
transported, carried onward and upward and outward into realms celestial. No need to struggle to
aid the operation—we release ourselves unto God.

One can be a student of the Scripture and yet not
be a partaker of the Divine Nature. It is the letter
that killeth but the SPIRIT MAKETH ALIVE!
What beautiful types unfold themselves as we read
the love story of Rebecca at the well! She received
her Isaac. When the Scripture says, "But as many as
RECEIVED HIM . . ." that is UNION WITH HIM.
I have united many couples in the bonds of holy
matrimony and I cannot remember one service in
which I did not use the words, "signifying that mys-
tical union between Christ and His Church," when
I pronounced the union of the couple who stood before me! When a bride becomes united to the man
of her love and choice, she loses *her identity.* She
takes his name, even as we take the Name of Christ!
She promises to love, honor and obey, even as the one
who becomes united to the Lord acknowledges Christ
as the headship of the Life.

Now, Rebecca was of marriageable age. She was
eligible. She was a serving Christian, so to speak, at
the wells of salvation. She was doing her duty and
performing her task well. But the fact of her eligi-
bility did not mean that she had already married. The
fact that we are doing things for Jesus does not of

necessity mean we are united to Him. The great moment came when the question was put to her, "WILT THOU GO WITH THIS MAN?" It meant turning her back upon, not only the past, but upon HERSELF. It meant the leaving of her old home and associations. It meant the changing of her name. It meant the releasing of her own body and will, for she was to be brought *under the authority of another*. There she was with all the qualifications of a bride, but not until she was released from her own self and will was she able to release herself to the bridegroom. Thus, the Heavenly Bridegroom is waiting for that company who, completely surrendered, will live alone for Him. "Hearken, O daughter, and consider, and incline thine ear; forget also thine own people, and thy father's house; so shall the King greatly desire thy beauty: for He is thy Lord; and worship thou Him!" (Psalm 45:10, 11)

POWER TO BECOME

We are interested in healing, and it is well that we are for our Father intended that we should be. Healing for body and for soul and for spirit! Healing that will cover every part of our being and our natures. Healing that in its divine surge will touch every extremity of our lives. First of all, then, we must avail ourselves of the imparted "POWER TO BECOME!" The power is given only to those who have "received HIM." Without Him, there could be

no "power." Apart from Him there is no power. The
Bride hath made herself ready by discovering in the
first place that in herself she could not get ready!
We receive power to become by discovering, first of
all, that in ourselves there is *no power to become!*
We are helpless: yet so many struggle and try to do
in self what only He has power to do. Only to "as
many as RECEIVED HIM" gave He the power. And
that power is inseparable from Himself. It is the
operation of His Presence; the unhindered flow of
His Life; the unhampered operation of His Will that
bears the genius of transformation and changes us
from what we are in self to what we can be in Him!
And it covers all of us: body, soul and spirit. "Know
ye not, that to whom ye yield yourselves servants to
obey, his servants ye are to whom ye obey; whether
of sin unto death, or of obedience unto righteousness?"

Our glorious Lord has purchased COMPLETE
AND PERFECT FREEDOM for His children! He
wants us to be rid of the chains of self and the bondage of the flesh-life. He wants us to enter into that
glorious liberty wherewith Christ hath made us free!
There is no yoke of entanglement of body or of soul
or of spirit that is pleasing to Him and in the operation of His love and grace He would deliver us from
them all. Even Death could not hold its prey, when
its prey was Life Himself! But, oh, how many bonds
we come with, in our futile struggles and endeavors
to liberate ourselves. "Loose thyself from the bands

of thy neck (will) O captive daughter of Zion!"
(Isaiah 52:2)

Our greatest enemy is SELF! Many proudly testify of their deliverance from sin and from specific
habits in meeting after meeting, but the most glorious and far reaching deliverance is the one from the
power of self. Who is Head? Does Christ have any
fellowship with Belial? Does Light have any communion with Darkness? As the bride submits to the
bridegroom and makes him her head, so the Bride of
Christ must relinquish her own headship of self and
will and become obedient to the One Whose Name
she bears!

ACKNOWLEDGE HIM

What healing miracles have been wrought in
body, soul and spirit in the lives of those who have
ceased from their struggles and, in all their ways,
have begun to ACKNOWLEDGE HIM! Is the
promise vain that He would direct our paths, if so
we did? Did He not conquer every adversary, not
only for Himself, but for us? Are not our bodies His
temples? The day was when some used to look upon
Divine Healing as akin to the waving of a "magic
wand" when we would receive a wonderful touch.
Something would be there one minute and presto, it
was not there the next! Now all this, under the
grace of God, was wonderfully true! Moreover it is
often true today. We cannot doubt what our eyes
have seen and our ears have heard. But I am con-

vinced that the Lord is opening to His children door-
ways through which we pass to our richer inheritance
as SONS AND DAUGHTERS OF THE LIVING
GOD! Partaking of the Divine Nature! Infused
with the Divine Life! Until body, soul and spirit
shall be so FILLED WITH HIM that we shall enjoy
and experience the freedom which He purchased. A
complete and a perfect freedom! A CURE that is
just as great as the CURSE!

DELIVERANCE

We have been born into the Body of God's dear
Son! We have been filled with the Spirit and we
have all surrendered to Him in various degrees. God
is requiring the "I will" and the "I do" to the WILL
OF THE FATHER! It is the Christ alone in us that
has pleased the Father. It is not a question of geogra-
phy alone. It is not, merely, "Is it the will of God
that I preach in China or in Wisconsin; in Africa or
in Louisiana?" It is not only the revelation of the
will as to what we shall do and where we shall be
externally. It is a far deeper thing than that! It is
our complete union with the Father through the Son
so that the Divine Flow may come into the Body of
believers; *and that* through Him we may receive
Resurrection power for spirit, soul and body.

In ordinary circumstances, when a case is given
over to a physician, he takes complete authority and
complete responsibility, only if his orders are followed

out implicitly. If the will of the patient supersedes
the orders of the physician, he will tell you that he
will accept no responsibility for the result. He insists
that the patient be moved to where he can observe
the case and give the proper diagnosis. Everything
contrary to the will of the physician is an impedi-
ment. Suppose the patient said to the doctor, "I am
determined to do such and such." The physician will
only permit such a thing to be done if it is in accordance with his plan. Everything is put into his hands:
the question of food, environment, exercise is all the
responsibility of the physician. More than once doc-
tors have walked out on cases where the patient insisted upon having his own way.

Should we make a less surrender to our blessed
Lord? Should there be anything less than a complete
yielding of plans and purposes of our own? It does
not, of necessity, mean the giving up of them, but
it does mean the surrender of them to His will. He
may give them back and if He does, it will be with
an increased power for we will not only have the joy
of going but of going in the center of His will. It is
far better to stay at home and do, seemingly, nothing
than to enthusiastically go outside His will. Remember that because we are called upon to do nothing,
it does not mean that nothing is done. A great deal
was accomplished on the night that Peter went to
sleep and did nothing and, methinks, such accomplishment was greater, by far, than if he had stayed

awake that night when he was in prison and tried to pick the lock! Christ is the great Liberator! He is our Freedom. He is our Deliverer! Is it not time we LET GO and entrust our lives to Him?

As with Rebecca and Eliezar, there was a ten day period before the start of the journey. It was a TIME OF PREPARATION. It was a time when there came the breaking of the bands that bound her to the past. It was the time of *preparation for separation,* so that when the final separation came it could be baptized in willingness and volitionary surrender!

HIS PROGRESSION

So it is there is PROGRESSION in our advancement Home to the Father! We have power to become children and if children then heirs; but we cannot expect to be heirs until we first become children. It is under our right as heirs of God that we experience the fullness of our Redemption. Perhaps, the hardest thing for most of us is the SURRENDER OF OUR WILLS. But what a glorious release there is when, at last, this is done. What a tremendous load of responsibility is lifted from hearts and minds which have been bewildered and lives which have been perplexed. It is, undoubtedly, true that the vast majority of God's dear children, who have not yet entered into the fullness of their inheritance, are consistently praying for the Lord to bless their wills! They plan *their* work and plan *their* meetings and

figure out what *they* want to do and then devoutly
kneel and ask God to bless them in the operation of
their wills. I am not saying that He does not do it,
for the immensity of His Grace is far beyond the
bounds of my understanding and concepts. His love
overwhelms me! But I do know that that is not God's
best. He is demanding of His children complete
obedience. The will of the Father operating always
in His Son Jesus is the PATTERN for the sons that
are coming forth. We cannot reach the infinite depths
of what was in the heart and mind of our blessed
Lord when He prayed beneath the olive tree, in the
garden! How He poured out His very heart before
the Father! And how the heart of the Father must
have gone out to the Son when in the closing part
of the prayer, He cried, "Nevertheless not My will
but Thine be done!"

That is what He wants from us! No matter how
right it may seem, "nevertheless not my will but
THINE be done!" No matter how desirable the
project; how fascinating the prospect, "nevertheless
not my will but THINE be done!" It is when we
come to full surrender that we are accepted as sons,
even as the Son was acceptable to the Father. Then
we are made HEIRS of God and joint-heirs with
Jesus Christ. The first radiant dawning of the glory
which shall be revealed in us, steals over the horizons
of the spirit; the world recedes and spiritual things
become nearer and dearer. God may demand obedi-

ence without giving His sons much light on the
"why" or the "wherefore." If we knew why—and
where—there would be no room for the exercise of
faith. Abraham believed God and it was accounted
unto him for righteousness. Not what he did, but
just what he believed. HE BELIEVED *GOD!* It was
because he believed God that he was willing, when
the time came, to answer to the call and GO OUT,
NOT KNOWING WHITHER HE WENT! There
was no hesitancy. He believed God! There was no
quibbling. He believed God! If he had known his
destination before he started, he would have walked
by sight and not by faith.

In natural journeys or progressions, we have an
understanding and then we proceed on our journey.
We get out our roadmaps; we compute the distances
between this place and that and figure what it will
cost us to travel from the place we are to the place
we want to be. But in our spiritual travel, we proceed by OBEDIENCE and FAITH! God does not
show His children the end from the beginning. He
simply says, "TRUST ME!" And we believe the
Lord, and it is accounted unto us for righteousness.
Not what we DO, but what we ARE! It is not the
act of obedience but the spirit of obedience which
pleases the Lord. Sometimes there could be no act
visible; there is no external manifestation, but there
is the operation of the Spirit working within. So it
is, we travel on such a path, walking by obedience

and faith and then the light illumines the pathway! This is the PATH OF THE JUST that shineth more and more unto the perfect day! It is on that road that we receive the fullness of our inheritance. There we come into the possession of those qualities of sonship that enable us to cry, "Abba, Father!" with the spirit as well as with the lips. Such children of obedience are, in reality, the SONS OF GOD! And in sonship there is wonderful, glorious freedom.

CHAPTER IV

THE LIGHT WITHIN

"They that are led by the Spirit they are the sons of God."

OUR SERMONS have been on, "BE FILLED WITH THE SPIRIT." We have emphasized the filling! We have talked about the indwelling. Now this is all very well, but the day has come when we are not only to be filled with the Spirit but be LED BY THE SPIRIT! We are not only to receive the Holy Ghost, but we are to give the government of our lives over to Him. He will direct them. He will be our Teacher. He will be our Guide. He will become the great Revelator and the Unfolder of the eternal Word! He touches the written Word and transforms it into life. He does within us what we can never do for ourselves. He imparts in a moment what we could never develop in self in a multitude of life-times. All He asks is that we yield ourselves to Him. He is the love gift of our loving Father. He does not want us to say, "Tell me what You will do with me before I make the surrender. Show me what the end of the path will be before I will break and yield my will."

He does not want us to ask the way. He wants us to believe Him. Jesus has already declared, "I am your Way. I am your Truth. I am your Life."

He said to Thomas, "Because thou hast seen Me, thou hast believed: blessed are they that have not seen, and yet have believed." (John 20:29) O, to love Him better than any earthly joy! O, to relinquish the reins of the government of life in the acknowledgement of our own dismal failures. Perhaps, the world has called us successful, but in our hearts we know how shallow such success has been. The fickle world cries, "Hosanna!" today, but "Crucify!" tomorrow. Is it too much that He demands when He asks us to live for HIM? Does He claim too much when it is His will that not in the Millennium, and not in some future age, but in the here and now, "the government shall be upon His shoulders?" When we walk in the Spirit we do not have to wait until the literal manifestation of the Reign of Jesus in the external is apparent to all the world. Man on the inside knows that "the wilderness and the solitary place will be glad for them and the desert shall rejoice and blossom as the rose." We can have that internally now. We experience in spirit the lying down together of the lion and the lamb. Natures become changed! The transforming power of the Christ operates in and through every vital part of our beings. Body, soul and spirit become permeated with the glory of His indwelling presence. The outflow of His Resurrection

Life reaches to the farthest extremity of our person-
alities and our lives are literally HID WITH
CHRIST IN GOD!

The fears about the future have taken the wings
of the morning and fled to the uttermost parts of the
earth. Despair is robed with joy and, here and now,
God begins to wipe all tears from our eyes. No longer
are we slaves to environment; no longer are we the
servants of circumstance. Christ is greater than
them all! They that are led by the Spirit, they are
the sons of God! Now, we may have a revelation
in the Scriptures and yet not RECEIVE HIM. We
may have an understanding of the Word, and yet not
experience the indwelling power and presence of the
Living Word.

Beloved, we must not stop to ask Him why. Let
us not demand to know the end of the journey before we start. He has said, "Blessed are they that
have not seen, and YET HAVE BELIEVED!" Even
the disciples had to *see* before they believed. But the
full reward, the highest Prize of the high-calling has
not been given to any other age! The fact of the law
of growth and progression prohibited that. It was
to the overcomers of the Laodicean age that He promised a seat on His throne. This is a most glorious
day. While civilizations and empires are collapsing,
the heavens are telling the glory of the Lord. What
a privileged people we are! We are living in the twi-
light hour of a dispensation. The Spirit of God within

is liberating us from our bonds and, one by one, they are breaking. Whom the Son sets free is free indeed.

THE LIGHT

When Gideon and his three hundred went out in the will of the Lord, there came a moment for the BREAKING OF THE PITCHERS, which liberated the light. Now the light was in the pitcher all the time, but the pitcher hid it. It was there, but the outside world could not see it. The pitcher knew it was within, but the light had not yet come to the FULLNESS OF MANIFESTATION. We must not forget that the light was in the little group of THREE HUNDRED, and not in the vast army which Gideon originally led! Every symbolic Scripture; every type in the Old Testament which points with unerring accuracy to the period of time in which we are now living declares the message of the called minority. Paul speaks of "the little company"—the remnant—the called out ones; the people who are willing to pay the price and to go all the way with God. I know it is sentimental and pleasing to the flesh to broaden and broaden the boundaries of the overcomers until all are included, but such is not the teaching of the Word. It is not the statement of the written Word and it is not the revelation of the Living Word.

In Gideon's three hundred of this day, the light is shining in the pitcher! We can see one another's

pitcher—the vessel—but we do not see the light. It
will not be long now. The light will soon be manifest!
The light which is even now within. And that light
is Christ: the glorious illumination of His indwelling.
The moment will come when God will speak from
Heaven! The pitchers will be broken. The outer
shell which hides the light will be touched by the
power of the Spirit and will fall away! Then will
come the shining of the Light of the world, the glory
of the Lord which shall be revealed in us. It does
not come by persuasion. All the growth and development of the Christ is taking place behind the veil of
the flesh and until the pitchers are broken, the mystery will continue to be veiled. But it is going on
just the same! This is something you cannot "preach"
people into; it is something you cannot persuade
people to receive. There must be the pull and operation of the Holy Spirit within in order that we may
enter into the fullness of our inheritance. We are
waiting for the Word! When He speaks, the veil of
the flesh will be taken away; the pitchers will be
broken and the light will be revealed which has been
shining there, by His grace, since the complete surrender was made. Remember the light is hidden but
"blessed are they that have not seen, and yet have
believed."

I have stated that we have now come to the most
complicated age of all; yet it is the most wonderful.
Our theology which should have helped us to God

has been a hindrance in that it has led us away from simple faith. We are more highly educated, perhaps, than at any other previous age, but we are more atheistically educated. We have begun to philosophize our experiences. We have more to undo and to forget when we come as little children to the acceptance of our Lord in simple faith.. Can we psychoanalyze Jesus? Can we take apart, with our philosophic tools, the rudiments of His saving grace? Can we measure God's mercy with our human minds, or fathom His illimitable love with our thinking? Evil men have waxed worse and worse; darkness is over the face of the deep. Confusion is everywhere. It is in every realm of life and thought. And yet now we have come to the age in which the Prize of the Full Redemption for body, soul and spirit is offered! Now is offered the Prize to the full overcomer! It is now, in these complicated, educated times that simple faith has been given power to become.

UNDERSTANDING

We are called upon to release the SELF BRAKES that the Holy Spirit might be given full authority and that we might grow, by His grace, and in His strength into the maturity of His indwelling. This message is not received through the reason; it comes to the heart. The understanding is not one of intellect. It is a spiritual concept. The knowledge of it is not that knowledge which is acquired by long hours

of study or through the processes of our classes and
classrooms. It is that knowledge which is born of
above; an IMPARTED knowledge which is part of
the ministry of the Spirit. Solomon did not pray for
an educated mind. He, rather, asked the Lord for an
UNDERSTANDING HEART! And the speech
pleased the Lord, for the Lord knew that the thing
for which Solomon prayed was greater than riches
and was mightier than the scepter which was held in
the hands of a king.

In the parable of the sower, the only ground
which brought forth was the good ground. "But he
that received seed into the good ground is he that
heareth the Word, and understandeth it; which also
beareth fruit, and bringeth forth, some an hundredfold, some sixty, some thirty." (Matthew 13:23) It
had to be good soil to bring forth even thirty, let
alone the sixty and the one hundredfold. The productivity of the seed is dependent upon the soil. It is
always good seed, for it comes from Him who is the
giver of every good and perfect gift. It comes from
the Author of Life. And He came that we might
have LIFE, and that we might have it more abundantly. He did not come that we might have death
and sickness and sorrow and pain. That was the result
of the Fall and part of the universal curse. But He
came from the Ivory Palaces, with His garments
smelling of myrrh and of aloes and of cassia to break
the bands of a fallen race and scatter the enemies of

human soul! He came to lead captivity captive and to give gifts unto the sons of men! He came to bring us *Emancipation* and this is exactly what He did! The seed which He sows is always GOOD SEED, but its generating power is limited to the degree of surrender and the consecration of the earth into which it falls.

"If ye be willing and obedient, ye shall eat the good of the land: but if ye refuse and rebel, ye shall be devoured with the sword: for the mouth of the Lord hath spoken it." (Isaiah 1:19, 20)

THE NEW DAY

The day was when I used to pray for power to become something and to do something. That day has gone. Today I pray for POWER TO BECOME NOTHING! I realize that self is the BRAKE that holds the power back. I know that if I surrender my life, He will give me His. Then this life, touched with depravity, robed in impotence, with a heart that is deceitful above all things, is swallowed up in the glorious majesty and power of His Resurrection Life. Talk about healing! It is there. Healing for body, and for soul and for spirit. Then it is that the "Sun of righteousness arises with healing in His wings." Then it is that the full impact of the promise, "I came that ye might have life and that ye might have it more abundantly," bursts upon the

soul with the full depth of its illimitable meaning.
We begin to feel the permeating influences of the
Spirit of Life in Christ Jesus which make obsolete
the laws of sin and of death! The physical body
responds to the flow of the Divine Life and pain and
suffering are gone in the light and power of His resurrection life.

So it is He is calling upon us to present our bodies
"a living sacrifice, holy, acceptable unto God," which
is our reasonable service. The brakes may be released
and the mechanism of the inner man may be placed
on the hands of One who understands. We cannot
produce the mechanism, but we can DRAG THE
BRAKES with our obstinate wills. We insist upon
knowing. We insist upon seeing. We insist upon having our own way on the ground that it is a good way.
We insist upon doing this because it is so reasonable
to the natural man. O, that we could enter into the
secret of that surrender in which His will will not be
questioned. "I delight to do THY will, O God!" No
man can delight to do the will of the Lord and yet
hang on to his own. How wonderful are the works
of the Lord in all the earth! Far past our human
understanding and far beyond the boundaries of the
operation of our thought. But His promises reach
from the center to the farthest circumference and
no part of us is excluded in the all-embracing scope
of His Redemption!

THE HANDMAID

It took centuries to bring forth the vessel of Mary, the mother of Jesus. Yielded and submissive soil after some 4,000 years of rebellion and disobedience under the Adamic headship! "Behold the handmaid of the Lord. Be it unto me according to Thy Word." There was surrender! There was obedience! She was willing to bear the stigma of being with child while she was yet in her virginity. She was willing to become, like her Divine Offspring, of no reputation. What glorious magnificence we find in those words, "Behold the handmaid of the Lord. Be it unto me according to Thy Word." There must be perfect obedience that the Seed of the woman might bruise the serpent's head. The promises of the Lord from the beginning of Creation were going to be fulfilled in and through her. In her submissive obedience, she received the Word of God, and became one with God, to bring forth the Son of God. How much more is He calling now the sons of God to yield themselves that they, too, might bring forth. For it is only in this HEAVENLY UNION which is symbolized by the marriage of people on earth, that the bringing forth will be brought about!

How fully persuaded was Mary that the letter— the Scriptures—contained this mystery? Did she have a complete and full understanding before the event of the miraculous conception? We think not! Rather, she received a Heavenly visitor and acquiesced to the Father's will. She was able to fulfill the requirements and the Holy Seed of the Father was received by a surrendered will in a body that God operated upon in the bringing forth of the Saviour of the world.

Of what use is it to pray when we still withhold our wills from Him Who loved us and gave Himself for us? Many have almost screamed themselves into hoarseness and into spiritual and physical exhaustion, importuning and pleading before the Throne of grace and wonder why the answer never comes. They thought they were waiting for God and, all the while, He was waiting for them. They have desired—but have they desired the will of God? They have asked— but has that asking been born of an operation of the Spirit within? We do not always know what to pray for, but the Spirit knows and sometimes He will pray for the manifestation of that within us "but for which, in our ignorance, we ourselves would never pray." Even a John the Baptist can feel the ground shaking beneath his feet when he finds himself in a situation that does not seem to fit into the Divine promise. If Jesus were the Son of God why did He allow John to be incarcerated for righteousness sake, in a prison cell? It was the human in John that said, "Art Thou He that should come or do we look for Another?"

But the question was answered. Nobody appealed with logic to John's reason. Nobody tried to persuade

him of the righteousness of his position or of the
integrity of his Lord. No one preached to him about
the sinfulness of his doubting and the inerrant ways
of his own thinking. Instead of that, Jesus spoke.
That was all. Everything was righted then. There was
no more question about it. Jesus spoke and the darkness was turned to light. The thing over which John
stumbled became a ladder up which he mounted
nearer to the heart of God and to the very gates of
Glory. And our blessed Lord knew all the time that
what John said was not really a revelator of what he
was. John had a little slip-back in his development.
It was a moment or two of struggle in his growth in
grace and in the unfolding purposes of His glorious
Lord. So Jesus spoke and the darkness was turned
to radiant light.

OUR CONFIDENCE

So we often find that not only the babes in Christ,
but often those who are baptized in the Spirit will
begin to question the judgments of the Lord. The
completely surrendered will and mind must reveal
the *outworking of the inwrought Christ*. One can
become a "believer" without becoming a "receiver"
of the INWROUGHT CHRIST as Lord of all! This
is the hour when the Lord is calling upon us to leave
all and follow Him. And leaving all means just that.
Absolutely all. He wants the surrender of heart and
life and mind and will! Everything must be laid at
the Master's feet and in all our ways we must

acknowledge Him. He, then, will direct our paths.

As "in My Father's house there are many mansions" so in our Adamic house are many prisons! We are often held by bonds and complexes. We are under the confining limitations of our flesh and quite often, seeing the mark of the high-calling in Christ Jesus, we cry as did one of old, "Who shall deliver me from the body of this death?" It is no use to struggle. Striving will never bring about the effect. Nothing that we could do in the way of attainment or accomplishment will ever bring to us the desired result. Our emancipation is in the Emancipator! Our deliverance is in the Deliverer! Our healing is in the Healer! Our salvation is in the Saviour! Come and reign, Jesus! Come and live within, blessed Lord! The end of the road of self-surrender is the beginning of the Highways of our God! And as we walk down that road, there is Health and Liberty; there is Freedom and Emancipation! And within our hearts there sounds a Voice sweeter than the sound of bells at even-tide, "Because I live, ye shall live also!"

And the sufferer on the sick bed, as well as the poor soul bound by the fetters of sin hears that declaration of His matchless love and grace and the shadows flee away. The long night is passed—the dayspring from on High has come at last. Deliverance is in the deliverer. Salvation is in the Saviour. Healing is in the Healer; Christ is in the Christian and the true Christian is hid with Christ in God.

CHAPTER V

THERE IS A RIVER

"There is a River, the streams whereof shall make glad the city of God, the holy place of the tabernacles of the Most High. God is in the midst of her; she shall not be moved: God shall help her, and that right early." (Psalm 46:4, 5)

THE ESSENCE of God, or the attributes of God, is as a River flowing! Now, we are the tabernacles of the Most High, and we are the city in which He rules and reigns. The streams of this River shall *make glad* the city of God and flow into and through the holy place of the tabernacles of the

Most High! "But the fruit of the Spirit is love, joy, peace, long-suffering, gentleness, goodness, faith, meekness, temperance: against such there is no law. And they that are Christ's have crucified the flesh with the affections and lusts." (Gal. 5: 22-24)

It is something *intangible!* It is beyond

human comprehension! It is outside the boundaries
of human understanding! It is in a realm of the
spirit in which the Holy Spirit alone can make manifest and bring in us the attributes of the Divine, the
fruit of the Spirit! It is the very ESSENCE OF GOD
flowing like a River! Against such there is NO LAW!
It requires the revelation of the Spirit to be understood. It is not of human works. It is not of human
effort. It is the unhindered and unhampered FLOW
of that River of His Divine Presence manifesting, not
humanity, but Diety! Not flesh; but the Spirit!

"Now the works of the flesh are manifest, which
are these: adultery, fornication, uncleanness, lasciv-
iousness, idolatry, witchcraft, hatred, variance, emu-
lations, wrath, strife, seditions, heresies, envyings,
murders, drunkenness, revellings, and such like: of
the which I tell you before, as I have also told you
in times past, that they which do such things shall
not inherit the Kingdom of God." (Gal. 5:19-21)
What a gulf there is between the works of the flesh
and the fruit of the Spirit.

After the Crucifixion and the Resurrection of our
blessed Lord, we find Him pleading, once again, with
the fisherman disciple, Peter. Listen to His words,
"Peter—son of Jonas—son of man—son of flesh—
lovest thou Me?" When our Lord used the word
"love" He spoke of the "agapos"—that River of DI-
VINE LOVE—the River-Love of God, which no
flesh, no Simon-son-of-Jonas could ever produce. It

was not as Peter, son of Jonas, that the disciple could know that love but only as PETER, SON OF GOD, through the transforming miracle of Calvary, and his being made nigh by the Blood! Flesh could not come up to that love! It could not rise above the filial love that sprang from itself. The love that Jesus wanted was not the love that flowed from the human heart; but the love that flowed from the River of the heart and essence of God.

If we try to produce in our natural flesh, the attributes of God, we rob Him. No matter how much we struggle so to do, we find all we can drink from is the MUDDY RIVER of our own flesh. The imitations we try to produce are not of the RIVER DIVINE in essence or in fruit. How we rob God when we struggle and endeavor to produce them from the river of self. The fruit of the Spirit are produced by the flowing of the River! This is the River, the streams whereof shall make glad the city of God, which we are, and the holy place of the tabernacles of the Most High, in which He dwells within. It is the unhindered and the unhampered flow of *His life* flowing through lives which have become *dead* to self and to sin, and bearing the fruitage of the manifestation of His presence.

"And they overcame him *by the Blood of the Lamb,* and by the word of their testimony: and *they loved not their lives unto the death!*" (Rev. 12:11) We are made eligible for this River of God

by, first, the cleansing of His Blood! There is no
other way! Self effort will not do. Human works,
however seemingly good, can never bring about the
result. Such cleansing is never attained through service. We see the crimson flowing stream from Calvary,
the Blood of God's pascal Lamb, cleansing us from
sin and making us eligible for the flow of the Divine
River. Secondly, we are made to know the life-giving
flow of this stream by being willing to come to "they
loved not their lives unto the death!" That is what
our Father asks of us. The muddy stream of self, and
the flow of the Essence of God, the clear, pure, crystal waters of His attributes cannot flow together
through the same river-bank. He calls to us, "Lovest
thou Me more than these?" We must enter with
Him into His death before we can know the power
of His Resurrection.

THE RIVER OF GOD

In our walk with Him, as sons, there is that purifying of the River of God. There is the flow of that
stream which manifests the attributes of God and
not the fruitage of self effort or of the labors of our
hands. The flow is intangible. It is not material. It is
of the Spirit! As we rise in spirit to walk with Him
in Heavenly places, we are made conscious of the flow
of His resurrection life in the beauty of its cleansing
healing power. The more we know of His Life—the
less we want our own.

If we love our lives, we are not able to die to them. What remains now is that FINAL LINK between the love of self and the Divine River of Love! Our Lord is calling upon us to let go until that link of self is broken and He receives us into that Life-giving stream! As it was with Peter, "You know I love You, Lord!" Is that the best that flesh can do? "Son of man, isn't there a little more that you can give Me?" There is a washing of regeneration that in the ultimate of God counts not its life dear. It is the final link. "And they loved not their lives unto the death!"

One can not take a *part* of a river and put it in a pitcher and say, "This is a river." The water ceases to be the river as long as it is removed from the river. It is not a case of our possessing something which we can contain in a little container of ourselves; but it is the manifestation of the Divine flow. It is the continuous flowing of the River, the streams whereof shall make glad the city of God. It is the fruit of the Spirit. It is the River of Divine Essence flowing! It is far beyond the possibilities of human attainment or the productivity of human goodness! It is LIFE DIVINE! Against such there is *no law!!* It means that we become wholly lost in God. The last link of the chain is broken and in the flow of this Life-giving stream, we withhold nothing but are able to say, "Yes, Lord, I love Thee more than these! And the love with which I love Thee is the Love Divine, the

Love of God!" We are never immune from the law of sin and death until we are wholly lost in God.

God is bringing us to the BREAKING POINT, where we love not our lives unto the death. We are coming to the passing over the gulf, wherein Heaven rejoices! "And *now* is come salvation and strength, and the kingdom of our God, and the power of his Christ: for the accuser of our brethren is cast down, which accused them before our God day and night." We are to be delivered from the accuser of our flesh. We are to be delivered from the bondage of this flesh-life. You ask the reason? The answer is because we have been WASHED IN THE BLOOD and LOVE NOT OUR LIVES UNTO THE DEATH! We are willing to be SUBMERGED in this Divine flow. We are willing to let go, and let God! We come to the END OF SELF, to the consciousness of the helplessness and the inability of flesh to produce anything but itself and to give the increase after its kind.

Our love will not do. Our synthetic peace will not suffice. It cannot produce the sweet, pure, crystal waters out of the impurities which we are! But, Oh, thank God, there is a RIVER, THE STREAMS WHEREOF SHALL MAKE GLAD THE CITY OF GOD! It is the River of the DIVINE ESSENCE. It is the River of His attributes—His love, His joy, His peace, and His longsuffering and it flows through the surrendered tabernacles of the Most High. It is not man struggling to live in God, but GOD LIV-

ING IN MAN! What rest and peace we know in the abiding presence of our Lord.

"Woe to the inhabiters of the earth and of the sea! for the devil is come down unto you, having great wrath, because he knoweth that he hath but a short time." (Rev. 12:12) And the dragon which is cast into the earth persecuted the woman bringing forth the manchild, but she is given the wings of an eagle, and out of the mouth of the serpent water comes forth as a *flood*, so that in that impure stream she might be overtaken and the dragon would carry her away! But the earth helped the woman, for the earth opened her mouth and swallowed up the flood which the dragon cast out of his mouth. And so into the wilderness she did fly!

Our Father is severing the SERPENT SEED from GOD'S SEED! He is delivering His sons from the floods of destruction to the River of God. When we are willing to count not our lives as anything, then the River of His love will cleanse and carry us on! In complete recognition of our own, inherent, fleshly weakness, we ask for His strength that the last ties of the self-life and the last chains of the flesh-life might be broken and that we might then experience the flow of the clear, crystal River which is GOD HIMSELF!

CONSTRAINING LOVE

The love of God constraineth us and we are carried into that place where to SEE GOD KILLS US!

O, this consuming power! This love of God! We stand overwhelmed in the midst of it! "Eye hath not seen, nor ear heard, neither have entered into the heart of man the things which God hath prepared for them that love Him!" (I Cor. 2:9) Love Him! Love Him more than life itself, and refuse to hold dear anything of flesh or of self! God hath prepared them! Prepared these unseen and unheard of things for THEM THAT LOVE HIM! But the Spirit is revealing them to us!

We are heirs and joint-heirs with Christ! O what a Redemption this! How far-reaching its implications and how glorious its fruit! To have the Spirit of God flowing through us and being so filled with the fruit of the Spirit, and cleansed from the attributes of the flesh, that at last we become PARTAKERS OF THE DIVINE NATURE, sharing not only in what He gives but in what HE IS, having the MIND OF CHRIST; knowing the beauty of HIS PEACE; being ravished with the FULLNESS OF HIS LOVE! "There is a River that makes glad the city of God!" It cannot make glad the flesh-life, for it will not flow therein! It cannot touch the self-life, for no pollution can enter its crystal-clear waters. It is the *supernatural life of God*, and we are the city that is made glad by the flowing of this River.

Our Adamic nature is A-DAM—an obstruction, obstructing the flow of the River Divine. There is a River, clear as crystal, that flows from the Throne of God! Not all of God's children have entered into this River. Not all have come to the place of complete surrender, but in these final days in the preparation of the Bride for the Bridegroom, many are feeling the call for the completely separated and surrendered life. No one is eligible for this River of Divine Essence unless they have been washed by the Blood of the Lamb and have opened wide the heart's door. Our Heavenly Father has sent the Spirit to CARRY US OVER INTO THE PROMISED LAND! As soon as we come to this River, our Adamic understanding obstructs. Self, perchance, would get in the way. Reason would hold us back. The last death struggles of a dying self would impede our being lifted into its healing, cleansing flow. But it is when we come to the END OF OUR UNDERSTANDING and are plunged into this River that we are carried out BEYOND! It passeth understanding! "And the peace of God, which passeth all understanding, shall keep your hearts and minds through Christ Jesus." You cannot put it in vocabulary! It is something that is *indefinable*. It is *intangible*. You can't say, "Do this and you have it!" It is the FLOW OF THE DIVINE RIVER! The FLOW OF THE LIFE OF GOD!

THE DIVINE ESSENCE

And so, in its healing, sanctifying, purifying stream, we are headed for the OTHER SHORE! Out into His Divine Essence! Cleansed continually!

Then from here on, it is just the essence of God flowing. The fruit is there. No struggle! The River just
flows! It is love, joy, peace, and longsuffering. Not
the product of our service or the labor of our hands;
but the very elements of the River Itself. Why should
we stand on the brink and allow our Adamic natures
to hold us back? Then the flood-tide of the dragon
that would hinder and stop us, coming out of the
mouth of the dragon, cannot any longer hinder, for
the earth eats up the venom of the serpent and we
continue on, cleansed, and carried on by the River of
God! (Rev. 12:15-16)

O, River Divine! River most glorious! We commit ourselves to Thee! Life of God! Attributes of
God! Very Essence of God, flow in us! Weary,
burdened soul, there is a River, the streams whereof
shall make glad the city of God, the holy place of the
tabernacles of the Most High!

CHAPTER VI

SOWING ABUNDANTLY

 *"But this I say, He which soweth sparingly shall reap also sparingly; and he which soweth bountifully shall reap also bountifully. E v e r y man according as he purposeth in his heart, so let him give; not grudgingly, or of necessity: for God loveth a cheerful giver. And God is able .to make all grace abound toward you; that ye, always having all sufficiency in all things, may abound to every good work."* (II Corinthians 9:6-8)

A S A DOCTOR proceeds in diagnosing a case to get down to the first causes of the ill, so the Spirit of the Living God, in Divine tenderness, would probe deeply into our hearts to see what may be the cause of our ills for spirit, soul and body. Even as we ask the Lord to bestow upon us His gracious gifts, we must also recognize that the Lord is asking us to

give our all to Him! The whole world is sick. Its
people are sick, and in a great majority of cases, God's
children are sick. Sick in body and in soul and in
spirit! What a needy people we are! But as we see,
on the one hand, the immensity of our need, we
behold on the other hand, A GOD WHO IS NOT
ONLY WILLING BUT ABLE TO MEET THAT
NEED!

So it is timely that we should inquire of the Lord,
"Diagnose my case, dear Lord, and let me know
wherein the failure has been in my contact between
my need and Your great supply." Wherein have we
failed? Why have not the measures of His grace
sufficed for our present necessities? Thus we turn to
Him, and ask Him for the revelation of the truth!

We are all familiar with the Scripture, "A double
minded man is unstable in all his ways." (James 1:8)
The Lord instructs us to seek Him with our WHOLE
HEART and to TURN COMPLETELY TO HIM!
It is out of the abundance of a man's heart that the
mouth speaketh. When the Spirit of the Living God
has sown the Word within our hearts, and we,
through our willingness of heart, have nourished and
cared for that which He has sown, we find the spiritual increase that He has promised. The seed of His
planting will bring forth a harvest, when with all our
hearts we nourish and care for it. We must keep in
remembrance, however, the necessity of the Spirit of
the Living God having His free course and access.

He wants us to be given wholly and completely to Him!

There is evidence on every hand and side these days, of the double minded man at work. We see the great lack in the attempts of men to bring about peace. We behold them preparing for war and yet crying, "Peace and Safety." There is no fixed policy. There is vacillation and turning from this way to that. The Lord has given us these external examples for our admonition, "upon whom the ends of the world have come."

"Why call ye Me Lord, Lord, and do not the things that I say?" Why do we have one word on our *lips* and our *hearts* are far off? Wherefore the Lord said, "This people draw near Me with their mouth, and with their lips do honour Me, but have removed their heart far from Me and their fear toward Me is taught by the precept of men." (Is. 29:13) It is not enough to call Him, "Lord," we must *make* Him Lord. It is not sufficient to see Him as King; but to KNOW HIM AS KING! To live, merely, nominally as a Christian is to have no channel through which His grace and love and power can flow to meet our needs in the time we call upon Him. It is the surrendered life that He can utilize. It is the yielded spirit through which He can approach and bring to us His all sufficiency which will meet all our need for body, soul and spirit.

THE TALENTS

In the parable of the talents, in Matthew 25:15, we read, "It is like a man who, when going on his travels called his servants and entrusted his property to their care. (*Weymouth*) To one he gave five; to another two, and to another one. Then comes the significant statement, "To each according to his capacity!" Our Lord is not asking us to do the impossible. The thing He requires of us can be done. Moreover He gives us grace to do it. He asks for the surrender of our lives, body, soul and spirit. All should be completely yielded to Him. It is when that complete surrender is made that we have a right to trust Him for everything that pertains to the life. Trust Him for the clothes we wear and the food we eat! "Take no thought for the morrow, what ye shall eat or what ye shall drink. Your Heavenly Father knoweth that ye have need of these things. But seek ye first the Kingdom of God and His righteousness and all these things shall be added unto you." We trust Him for healing in case of sickness and for the maintenance of health in these physical bodies. We believe Him for the flow of His Resurrection Life. But can we believe that His Resurrection Life will flow into a life that has not been surrendered? Can we withhold our life from Him and expect Him to care for it? And yet we know that is just what so many do and then begin to turn to each other for help, instead of realizing that ALL OUR HELP

COMETH FROM THE LORD! Nought that we have we call our own! We owe it to the Giver! What He has given us, we must utilize. The talent that He has imparted, we must invest. If we keep our lives, we lose them. We must learn to SOW ABUN-DANTLY! We must learn to LAVISH OUR AF-FECTIONS UPON HIM! When we refuse to pour out, we make it impossible for Him to pour in.

He is calling, "My son—My daughter, give Me thine heart!" And the heart is more than lip service. It is the seat of the affection and the emotion. It is the center of the personality which we are. He wants all of us and it is when we give ourselves, unreserv-edly, to Him that we behold how unreservedly, He has given Himself to us. We must make that surren-der. Wherever there is human reservation, there is always a limited crop. That which is reserved of self is that which is without faith; and that which is without faith is sin. We cannot expect the harvest, unless the seed is put in the ground!

Perhaps there are some who rebel and find fault because there are others who have sown extrava-gantly in their love for God. Whenever they are approached about a complete consecration or sur-render they say, "Do you think I am going to think about the Lord *day and night?* I have so many other things to do in life. I pay tithes and I go to prayer meeting on Wednesday night and attend the church services on Sunday and I do my best to live right and

I think that is all the Lord requires of me." That
seems to be a popular concept of the requirements
our Lord is making upon His children, but it is far
from the truth. Whether we eat or drink, we should
do all to the glory of God! The surrender of heart
and life—of past, present and future—of all that we
have and all that we are—into His tender care and
keeping, is the type of surrender our Lord is asking
of His children. He prefers our LOVE to our SERV-
ICE and the adoration of the heart more than mere
worship of the lips. How can we withhold when He
has given His all for us?

THE HARVEST

Remember, there is a HARVEST TIME! "Be
not deceived, God is not mocked, for whatsoever a
man soweth that shall he also reap. But he that soweth to his flesh shall of the flesh reap corruption; but
he that soweth to the Spirit shall of the Spirit reap
life everlasting." (Gal. 6:7) Can we expect an abundant harvest when we refuse to sow an abundant
crop? Can we expect to *receive* lavishly when we fail
to *give* of our self lavishly? Can we expect ALL OF
HIM when we refuse to give Him ALL OF US? Our
main business is not to live but to LIVE FOR HIM!
It is in living for Him and in Him that we enter into
the fullness of His own Resurrection Life! We must,
in actuality, SEEK FIRST THE KINGDOM! And
what is the Kingdom? It is coming ultimately into

the inheritance of all that Christ purchased upon Calvary including the redemption of the body. If in all our ways we acknowledge Him and in all our days we love Him and adore Him and, thereby, sow the seed of the Spirit, how abundant will be the harvest! For only He can bring about that harvest. Paul may plant and Apollos may water but God Himself gives the increase!

Many people feel it sufficient for their spiritual health to look in the Bible at certain intervals and only in time of need, search the Scriptures for the issues of life. They rather regard the One, who is a present help in time of trouble, as Someone to whom they should go *only* in time of trouble. They would utilize the Lord in time of their need. They recognize His supply; but never approach it except when they need it. How impoverished such a soul is! How vastly different that is from the EXTRAVAGANT LOVE that He pours out upon us! So extravagant was it that while we were yet sinners, He loved us! It was HIS LOVE which drew us from our sins; and Love guided the nail-pierced hand that in tenderness lifted the scales from our eyes that we might behold Him. But in His gifts, He is never coercive! He does not force us to love Him, or to follow Him, but He calls us and, in surrender and in willingness of heart, we count it all joy to do what He asks us to do. We find that if we love Him, we are drawn to Him with cords of love.

The disciples on the Emmaus road, that day, did not know the identity of the Stranger who walked by their side. But He radiated love! There was something about His very presence that impelled them to invite Him to spend the evening when the day was fast spent. In telling of it later they said, "Did not our hearts burn within us as He walked with us in the way?" Has your heart burned as He walked with you? Or is your prayer life a "chore"? Is the hour which you spend in His presence something that you have to "set apart" in a sacrificial way because you think it is, merely, the right thing to do? Is it a burden too heavy to bear that we carry the seed of this deliverance message in our hearts? Are not His words sweet, soothing, energizing; gentle as bells at evening pealing? Or is it a task that we face with a spirit of the man who approaches some part of his daily labor, rolling up his sleeves, and saying, "Here goes!" Remember as we sow, so shall we reap. If we would enjoy the harvest, we must first plant the seed.

THE OPEN WINDOWS

Bring ye all the tithes into the storehouse and see if He will not open the windows of heaven and pour out such a blessing you will not be able to contain it! Prove Me, now, saith the Lord! Think not that He was speaking merely of money or of worldly possessions, when these words were uttered. Perhaps, we would use them less as our favorite text in inducing people to give of their worldly goods for the work of the Lord, if only we put them in their broader and larger setting. It includes our worldly possessions, but it also includes our SELVES. It means the surrender of body and of soul and of spirit! What He would have us do is to lose our lives completely, for HIS SAKE, and losing them, WE FIND THEM. They are not our lives to keep. They do not belong to us. He purchased them. He redeemed them. We, sentimentally, sing that we are "masters of our destiny and the captains of our soul," when the truth is that we are no such thing. Am I the captain of my barque? Can I ignore God and claim that such a one as I, who was born in iniquity is "the captain of the soul?" Such a statement may well be made in a time of temporary calm; but when the storms begin to blow and the tempest comes, we admit and recognized our appalling helplessness. It is then that such would turn to the Captain of their salvation and cry, like Jonah did: "Salvation is of the Lord!" Not of self; nor of self-will; not of one's own desire or of traveling to the "Tarshish" of one's choosing. Salvation is of the Lord! And of Him alone. We must come to complete surrender—our homes, our lives, our hearts—all are His! As He died for us, we live for Him. Then the one who gives lavishly receives lavishly. The one who gives abundantly receives abundantly. Until we give our all to Him, we may read about Him giving His all to us, but we will

never know the joy of the fullness of experience. It
is the POURED OUT LIFE which can experience
the LIFE POURED IN! "The liberal soul shall be
made fat and he that watereth shall be watered also
himself." (Prov. 11:25)

The liberal soul counts itself as NOTHING
that it might win Christ! The soul of such a one
reaches out in abandonment of self and finds that it
touches the riches of God, the reservoirs of Divine
supply. Those "reservoirs" are tapped when we "pull
the plug of self." How easy it is to choke the chan-
nels! We pray for God to help while at the same
time we hinder. Letting go and letting God brings
God NIGH! That which withholdeth suffereth lack.
"Cast thy bread upon the waters; for thou shalt find
it after many days." (Eccl. 11:1) Your bread could
be your substance or it could be your life and soul.
In order to receive it you have to give it away! The
program of the Lord is not the philosophy of this
world. We say, "keep and have"; but the Lord says,
"Give and receive!" The more you give of self and
of love and of adoration, the more you receive of Him
and then the more you have to give, and giving the
more, you receive the more and so the cycle goes on
and on until our lives become filled with all the fullness of God.

THERE IS NO LACK

The world calls us foolish when we abandon ourselves to God; but the Lord says such a one will never

suffer lack. David said, "Once I was young, but now I am old; but I have never seen the righteous forsaken, nor his seed begging bread." "My God shall supply all your need according to His riches in glory by Christ Jesus." And again in Psalm 34:10, we read, "The young lions do lack and suffer hunger, but they that seek the Lord shall not want any good thing." Remember that the good things of which He speaks cover every part of our nature and apply to every department of our lives. It means being lifted when we have fallen; comforted when distressed; healed when sick; kept through adversity and guided through every trial. As we give Him all we have and are, so He meets the need for all we have and are. Give unstintingly! Give lavishly!

If we reap sparingly, is it because we have sown sparingly? We have withheld self and that is why we receive sparingly! We have thought we had to hold the authority over self! When we are released from self, the Living Waters flow continually. In the beginning Adam "dammed up" the Divine flow which was without beginning and without ending! The stream was there, but disobedience stopped the flow. Anything that tries to "barter" with God and hinder His life flowing fully for body, soul and spirit is an OBSTRUCTION! Adam through disobedience became an obstruction to the flow of those Living Waters and for 6,000 years such obstruction has brought sin and sickness and death to the human family. If we would have that flow returned, we who left in disobedience must come back in obedience. That is why the *precepts* are attached to the promises! That is why He who so freely would give to us would have us give just as freely to Him. But oh, how little is our giving in comparison to the fullness of the abundance of His giving! What we surrender is forgotten in the immensity of the flow of what He releases to us. Nature cannot begin, with her law of the harvest, even though it be one hundredfold to compare with the increase that comes to the man who gives the Lord his broken and his contrite heart.

HE IS ABLE

It was necessary for Jesus to come to this earth and to take upon Himself the form of a man and to be tempted in all points like as we that He might succor us that come unto God by Him. He, the Son, deals with the Father on our behalf as One who understands what it is to walk in the flesh; as One who knows the pull of the flesh-life that the sons of Adam endure. He listened to the scornful epithets which unbelieving human lips hurled at Him! He received the cruel barbs of their criticism and knew the physical suffering and the pain that iniquitous, selfish, fleshly men could impart. And because He, Himself, has suffered in the flesh, He is able to succor all those that are found in fashion as men. He knew what it was to be homeless. He knew what it was to be hungry. He participated in our infirmities! He shared in the deepest and darkest of our testings and trials; yet He came to share in them that He might become our WAY OUT! Think not that He would ask us to do the impossible! When He says in all thy ways acknowledge Him, He means in all ways—in everything—and in return, He promises to guide and to keep in every department of life. What a glorious exchange He would give us! Where we say, "All that I have is Thine," we know in return that He says to us, "And all Mine is thine." What an exchange! What have we to offer, beside the love of our heart which He cherishes the most. We come with our broken bodies and, in exchange He gives us His health. We come with our sin and He gives us His holiness. We come with our darkness and, lo, He becomes our Light! We come with our misunderstanding and misinterpretation, and we adore Him as the revealed Truth of God! What an exchange! Why should we withhold! Why should we want to keep back any minute part of His purchased possession? He became US, that we might become *HIS DWELLING PLACE!*

Ruth lay at the feet of Boaz all through the night. When she was betrothed to him, she went out to glean no more! When we set our love upon Him, He covers us and watches over us. This is the night of the world's affairs and we are feeling the need of God's care and protection in this needy hour. How wonderful to feel ourselves at our Boaz' (our Christ's) feet! Could any comfort and consolation be greater than this, to know that we are covered and protected and in UNION with Him. It is the rich soul, indeed, that is "all out for God," with no reservations at all. Then when He leads us to "Go," it is a joy when it is HIS APPOINTMENT. He wants us to FLOW IN HIM, knowing that whatsoever we do He is directing, and then we can do it with all our hearts. There is no withholding. We are so impoverished in our pinched lives, doling out this and that. But all Glory wants to lavish upon us the fullness of God's love! All Glory is waiting to bestow the riches of His grace through Christ Jesus! So lavishly! Hold nothing back! How great has been His gift to us and how all comprehensive His benefits. "Who healeth *all* thy diseases and who forgiveth *all* thine iniquities!"

THE LOVE DIVINE

We have known people who have been on their beds of sickness and have tried to "make a deal" with God. We have heard them say, more than once, "Lord, if You will raise me up, I will serve You. If You will heal me, I will do this or I will do that." Poor souls! What they need is not a touch in body, but a revelation of the LOVE OF CHRIST that will so break them in heart and in spirit that they will lay their lives at His blessed feet. How many are misers when it comes to God! They want their way; their lives! They want everything, but how much are they willing to give to Him! We pray to Him for health, but have we not heard Him pray, as it were, to them, "My son—my daughter— give Me thine heart!" Can we approach the Father's throne except through Christ? He is the ONLY DOOR! If we come up some other way, we are thieves and robbers and are we not thieves and robbers when we withhold from God that which is rightfully His? And that means our bodies—souls and spirits. He gave His life to purchase them. He died to redeem them. They are HIS and not ours, and we have no business to withhold them or any part of them from His loving care and His tender keeping. Freely we HAVE received; may God give us grace to FREELY GIVE!

In Bethany, in the long ago, the fragrance of some ointment filled the room and its rich aroma has never died away. The woman broke the alabaster box of the precious ointment at His feet. For it, she was criticized. They said, "This is gross waste." But she knew there was nothing too expensive for His burial. That ointment was the most extravagant thing—the most precious thing, she had; but the most extravagant thing and the most precious thing that God had was His only begotten Son. He was being sacrificed upon the Cross of Calvary—the Just for the unjust! The woman with the alabaster box knew that the most extravagant thing she could do would be small. The Saviour said, "She has done this for My burial and she will always be remembered for the breaking of this box. She has done it in remembrance of Me." His life was to be extravagantly spilled for the life of the world. He was to be slain and His blood spilled and His life poured out that we, in our sickness and poverty, might have that Virtue flowing in abundance unto us. How dare we, in the face of that fact, begin to "bargain" with God! Can we say, "I will do this for YOU—if—if You will do this for me." More than once we have seen the flow of His fulfilled promises sweep over body, soul and spirit when the heart has cried, "All to Jesus, I surrender; all to Him I freely give."

LOVEST THOU ME?

Our Lord tried long to get an extravagant answer from Peter. "Lovest thou Me more than these?" And Peter answered with the "fileo" love which means, "I am very fond of you." But that did not satisfy the hunger and the thirst of the spirit of the Christ. He did not want that partial love. He did not want the disciple for whom He had done so much merely to be willing to go part of the way. So again, He cried, "Lovest thou Me?" And again Peter answered; but it was not sufficient. And indeed it never was sufficient. How the heart of Christ must have grieved when Peter did not pour out his all. What Jesus wanted to hear was "Yes Lord, with my whole heart and soul I love Thee."

The King of Glory is starving for an EXTRAVAGANT LOVE! I believe He would rather have the complete love of the hearts of sinners whom He has redeemed than listen to the music of the angels, singing His praise around the glassy sea! No word is sweeter in His ears. His Bride is not to be taken from a company of angels; but from redeemed sons of men who have SOLD OUT TO GOD, and surrendered their all at His blessed feet. The eyes of the Lord run to and fro through the whole world to show Himself strong on behalf of those whose hearts are perfect toward Him! The perfect heart is that in which dwelleth EXTRAVAGANT LOVE. It withholds nothing but gives back to Him all that we are, because we belong to Him. Is there anything that kills the Spirit so much as the manifestation of indifferent love? It is not merely a command, it is an appeal from His heart. "Love the Lord thy God with all thy heart—and with all thy soul and with all thy mind—and all thy strength!"

From us there trickles that little stream of our love! Small it is, indeed, but it is all that we have and all that we are. Then like bread cast upon the waters, it returns, and it is a flood-tide of grace and glory. It is all we need—all we need.

In short, the whole of His written and revealed Word is leading us to one thing. Do not merely believe it! Do not mentally accept it as a creed! Do not take it as a loftier ideal to contemplate but BE IT! Become it! BE ENTIRELY HIS! And He is the living Word.

CHAPTER VII

RUN TO WIN

"I will instruct thee and teach thee in the way which thou shalt go: I will guide thee with Mine eye!" (Psalm 32:8)

I SAW A GARDEN planted with good seed. It was carefully fertilized. It had a good sprinkling system, and in the beginning everything was done to make it a successful garden. But the gardener became occupied with other things and the weeds began to take over! Now they have grown so high that the product of the good seed has been buried and overshadowed by the growing of the weeds. Even so in us, the weeds may take over in the last hour of the race!

So the call of the Lord is to RUN TO WIN! RUN TO WIN! Not just to be running, but to win the Prize. It is so easy to drift along with the crowd. This is not a call to the masses of men but to those who want TO WIN! If we want to win we must RUN TO WIN! Our Father will give us time for the things of life, but the important thing now, in this crucial hour, is that we run to win! The Prize

comes when we TOUCH CHRIST! It is then that
life springs forth! It is then that we KNOW HIM!

It is the "make haste" time. It is time for us to
be in the FLIGHT OF GOD! There is speed and
rhythm in such a flight! We must needs beware of
the danger of that which Paul, the seasoned warrior,
warned young Timothy, "For the time will come
when they will not endure sound doctrine: but after
their own lusts shall they heap to themselves teachers,
having itching ears; and they shall turn away their
ears from the truth, and shall be turned unto fables!"
(II Tim. 4:3, 4) God, our Father, is sending forth
warnings and instructions for His sons that they
might be DISCIPLINED SONS and not disobedient
to His direction.

"In the multitude of words there wanteth not
sin: but he that refraineth his lips is wise." (Proverbs
10:19) In the multitude of words, we lose the ES-
SENCE OF GOD! It is not our words that are to
bring forth in this time, but it is the PERFORM-
ANCE OF GOD! "Blessed is she that believed for
there shall be a performance of those things which
were told her from the Lord!" (Luke 1:45) Now,
God is showing forth on every hand and side His
illustrations of the truth. People are dying because
of the words of man—vain talk and idle words—
words—words—words! "Ye have wearied the Lord
with your words. Yet ye say, Wherein have we wearied Him?" cried the prophet Malachi. The empty

conversations are sapping the life and the vitality of God's children and bringing in roots of bitterness and misunderstanding and many are defiled thereby! But the Lord has said, "The words that *I* speak unto thee, they are Spirit and they are Life!" It is time to make way for the WORD OF THE LORD in the inner being, for God is now speaking and He would even create the fruit of our lips!

In the words of royal wisdom given by the King of heaven to a spiritually hungry king of Israel, we find the direction that leads us to health both of body and of spirit. "Trust in the Lord with all thine heart; and lean not unto thine own understanding. In all thy ways acknowledge Him, and He shall direct thy paths. Be not wise in thine own eyes: fear the Lord, and depart from evil. IT SHALL BE HEALTH TO THY NAVEL, AND MARROW TO THY BONES." (Proverbs 3:5-8) How He longs to lift the burden—How He yearns to set us free.

The days of His appearing are in the earth! "And as it was in the days of Noah, so shall it be also in the days of the Son of man. They did eat, they drank, they married wives, they were given in marriage, until the day that Noah entered into the ark, and the flood came, and destroyed them all. Likewise also as it was in the days of Lot; they did eat, they drank, they bought, they sold, they planted, they builded; but the same day that Lot went out of Sodom it rained fire and brimstone from heaven, and destroyed

them all. Even thus shall it be in the day when the
Son of man is revealed. In that day, he which shall
be upon the housetop, and his stuff in the house, let
him not come down to take it away: and he that is
in the field, let him likewise not return back. Remember Lot's wife. Whosoever shall seek to save his
life shall lose it; and whosoever shall lose his life shall
preserve it." (Luke 17:26-33) God is asking us with
what are we occupied today. We can see a parallel
picture between the times pictured above and the
time in which we live. "They did eat, they drank,
they bought, they sold, they planted" etc. They were
occupied with the business of the earth! And yet
where today, except in the hearts of the children of
the Lord, do we find life and peace and joy? There is
more money than ever before and yet, less happiness!
Men possess more of the power to buy and yet the
world was never filled with more of misery and sorrow and suffering! Although they talk of peace, in
actuality, there is less peace, because they have elim-
inated the Author of peace.

So it is in these days of the coming of the Son of
man! In those olden times, only Noah and eight souls
who took seriously the Presence and Instruction of
God Almighty were saved! Noah was termed an old
fool! The foolishness of Noah turned out to be the
wisdom of God. What is God's definition of a fool?
A fool is a man who has said in his heart that there is
no God! And because there is no God, he cannot and

will not obey the instructions of God. The wise man is he who builds upon the Rock, before the storm ever breaks and then when the storm breaks, he is able to ride through the gale!

HIDDEN WITH CHRIST

We are to see a reversal of strength. The strong of today will be the weak of tomorrow and the weak of today will be the strong of tomorrow! Not many mighty, nor noble have been called. Our Heavenly Father hath chosen the weak things of the world to bring to nought the things that are! We are going out of the RULE OF MAN and are entering into the RULE OF GOD. When the Lord reigns by His Spirit, no flesh shall glory in His Presence! "For ye see your calling, brethren, how that not many wise men after the flesh, not many mighty, not many noble, are called: but God hath chosen the foolish things of the world to confound the wise; and God hath chosen the weak things of the world to confound the things which are mighty; and base things of the world, and things which are despised, hath God chosen, yea, and things which are not, to bring to nought things that are: that no flesh should glory in His presence." (I Cor. 1:26-29)

We are being REDUCED TO GOD! It is there that we find life and health and joy and peace! It is there that we discover longsuffering and meekness and come in vital contact with the nature of God

Himself. In this operation, one is found, in the final
state, HIDDEN WITH CHRIST IN GOD!

In the parable of the virgins, we read, "But the
wise answered, saying, Not so; lest there be not
enough for us and you: but go ye rather to them that
sell, and buy for yourselves." (Matt. 25:9) It is time
to buy! GO BUY! That means that it is time to
DO BUSINESS WITH GOD IN THE SPIRIT! It
is high time that we made the necessary preparations
for His appearing! To the rich man, Jesus said, "Go
sell all that thou hast and give to the poor." He *was*
rich in this world's goods; but also in self. The prin-
ciple business with which we can be really occupied
in this fleshly tabernacle is that of SELLING OUT
AND BEING FILLED WITH GOD! His command
has been, *"Slay utterly!"* The internal Amalekites
must be exterminated and the fleshly kings must be
put to death. We have heard the cry, "Slay utterly"
but have we obeyed? We cringe from giving up
that which we possess in order that we might experience the fullness and the richness of the promises!
II Corinthians 8:9 tells us "For ye know the grace
of our Lord Jesus Christ, that, though He was rich,
yet for your sakes He became poor, that ye through
His poverty might be rich." The heart must be the
dwelling-place of the Eternal! We must guard our
hearts for out of the fullness of the heart the mouth
speaketh. No longer should we follow the law of sin
and of death but we should become obedient to the

law of the Spirit of life in Christ Jesus. If we follow the Spirit of Life, then the body will prosper even as the soul prospers.

HIS TEMPLES

Our bodies were made to become the temples of the Living God and God Himself would cleanse those temples. He would cleanse us from our words, our ways and our works, that out of our innermost beings might flow rivers of Living Water. When He said this He spake of the Spirit Whom He would send and the Spirit was to indwell men and flow like a river of Divine grace and glory through them! Does not the physical wound teach us that because of the corruption lying below the surface, healing must start from deep within? Healing of the wounds on our physical bodies comes, not from the *outside inward*, but from the *inside outward*. Yet much of our teaching has had to do with the external. Christians have been taught, for instance, to abstain from all *appearance* of evil. Now this is a Divine injunction, but we cannot isolate this text and take it out of its setting. We may abstain from all appearance of evil and yet, in the innermost being, we may be filled with dead men's bones! Though we may appear on the outside as a Christian, yet the inner man may be crying, "Woe is me, for I am undone; because I am a man of unclean lips, and I dwell in the midst of a people of unclean lips: for mine eyes have seen the King, the Lord of hosts." (Is. 6:5)

It takes the vision of His holiness and His purity to bring to us the vision of our own impurity. As the camel could not go through the eye of the needle but, of necessity, must unload at the gates of Jerusalem before entering the city, even so must a rich man—rich in self—also unload all of the things by which he is made rich, as an Adamic man. For such a life makes us poor in the things of the Spirit. Our Father wants us to become rich in spiritual things and self must decrease in order that He might increase.

OUR REDEMPTION

All things point to His imminent coming! The appearing of the Lord is nigh! When at last He comes will He find that room within us for HIMSELF? Is there room in us for HIS FAITH? Is there room for HIS WILL and for HIS WAY? The cry has gone out in this midnight hour, "Behold the Bridegroom cometh!" It is time that we made way for the King! Let us make straight paths for the Lord! He is coming to manifest Himself in the temples of clay. He hears our cry, "We are sick, O Lord!" There is one thing to do and that is to MAKE WAY FOR HIM! Healing radiates from the wings of the Sun of righteousness like the rays of the morning sun! He remembers our frame. . He knows that we are dust, and He understands our frailities and our weaknesses. We are *not* sufficient; but He *is!* In the midst of the perplexity and adversity on every hand and side, the

cry has come, "Look up, for the time of your Redemption draweth nigh!" It will be a full Redemption! A Redemption for BODY, for SOUL, and for
SPIRIT! And this is the hour when it can be said, of
a truth, "IT DRAWETH NIGH!" Let us not then
be overly concerned with earthly things and the cares
of this life lest that day come upon us unawares!
Let us keep our hearts and minds on heavenly things.

Because of our yearning for the fleshpots of
Egypt, digestive organs cannot take the heavenly
manna, much less the corn of the new Land of
Promise. Men have become so used to the food of
the days of their bondage in Egypt that the manna
which falls from heaven is, at first, distasteful to
them. Like Israel in the wilderness they begin to cry
out for the old food; the old things; the old ways;
the old ideologies and the old philosophies! If the
spiritual digestive organs cannot take manna, how
much less will those organs be able to digest the corn
of the New Land when at last we enter into the fullness of our inheritance. *The new wine cannot be put
in the old bottles!* God wants to implant within us
the new creation life. There must be no part of the
old left. He deals with the inner man and there is the
casting out of the bondwoman and her child that
there might be room for the Isaac, the Child of
Promise! Adulterations have never been pleasing to
the Lord and they certainly are not conducive to the
development of the sons of God. It will not be part

of the world and part of heaven; part of flesh and
part of the Spirit; part of human nature and part
of Divine nature! "As many as are led by the Spirit
of God they are the sons of God."

IN TUNE WITH GOD

How easy it is to be TUNED TO ONE AN-
OTHER and not IN TUNE WITH GOD! It is
little wonder that we fail to hear His voice when the
controls of the spirit are tuned in to so many fleshly
enterprises and utterances! When you have two pro-
grams coming over the air at the same time from the
same radio, neither of them mean anything at all and
the listener is left in confusion. The cry has gone
through the Camp, "Choose ye this day whom ye will
serve!" We have been tuned too much to our own
desires and to each other but we must be IN TUNE
WITH GOD! When the herald of His Coming at
last sounds forth, we want to be on the wave-length
and the beam which will let us hear it!

Doing "the best we know how" is not good
enough! Jesus would never have had to die at Calvary's Cross if the best we could do was, in reality,
good enough. The truth is that we insult our God
if the "best we can do" is offered to Him! It is not
the best that *we* can do but the best that *He* can do!
"Then shall we know, if we follow on to know the
Lord: His going forth is prepared as the morning;
and He shall come unto us as the rain, as the latter

and former rain unto the earth." (Hosea 6:3) This is the race we are running. We must RUN TO WIN! We must RUN TO KNOW CHRIST! This is why we have to "sell out" completely to God. Christ sold out when He left His heavenly glory to bring us back from bondage, even as in days of old the children of Israel were led from slavery to the gates of the Promised Land! No wonder the "best we can do" is not good enough! To say that we are doing the best that we can is to place ourselves back in that state of "the woman did tempt me and I did fall!" Our only hope is in Him! He Himself is our Salvation! He is our Wisdom! He is our Strength! He is our Healing! He is our all and in all!

"He shall call upon Me and I will answer him; I will be with him in trouble; I will deliver him and honour him. With long life will I satisfy him and show him My Salvation!" (Psalm 91:15, 16) He has come to show us His Salvation and to satisfy us with long life! And not only has He come to *show* us His Salvation, but He has come to INDWELL us and to BE our salvation, and the life He imparts is the Resurrection Life that He brought in triumph and victory over death and the grave!

We have perhaps, run along the avenues of pleasure, seeking for peace, but never finding it, because there is no peace outside His Presence! We have imagined we could find release and escape from the yearning spiritual hunger within us by indulging in those things "which the Gentiles seek" only to find ourselves as hungry and as empty as we were when the search began. It is not even how many hours we spend in a church, necessarily, but how many hours, day and night, is our inner chapel opened at that gentle knock, "May I come in and sup with you and reveal Myself unto you?" Or have we become too preoccupied with the nonsense of the world to catch the cadence of that Voice, when at last He speaks? Compare the time we spend in the presence of the Lord, opening our hearts for the revelation of the realities of God with the time we spend in frivolity and the indulgence in those things which do not add one iota to our spiritual growth! When, perchance, in some experiences listening to the voice of God is endured for a time, we then lapse back into the foolish things of an unregenerate world!

HE WILL ENTER

No matter what occupation one may have, be it minister or contractor; carpenter or pruner of trees, if the door of the heart is ajar for Him, God will enter and illustrate to us, so that it will be one continual revelation of Himself. Paul, the tent-maker, said; "For me to live is Christ!" That meant in making tents, as well as the preaching of the gospel from the pulpits of Macedonia. Be it on the sick bed or in the daily labor of our vocation, we must continually be DOING BUSINESS WITH GOD! How

He loves to enter in and take possession of the inner man, revealing Himself and His truth until the glory of that apocalypse and revelation supersedes all of the values of the world outside. Then it is we can say, "For me to live is Christ and to die is gain." Yes, death to the nonsense and inconsequential things of this life!

Our Father knows that we have need of food, clothing and shelter. He has promised that if we SEEK FIRST the Kingdom of God and His righteousness all these other things will be added unto us. Jesus Himself told us where that Kingdom was. It is *within.* It is there He would reign and He who feeds the sparrows can give His children bread! In all our ways, if we acknowledge Him, He has promised to direct our paths! As many as are led by the Spirit of God they are the sons of God.

It would do us good to take inventory and see how much of unnecessary earthly pursuits and unnecessary detail fills our life. If there could be erected before our spirits a screen of our own consciousness so that we could see a photograph of the past 24 hours, and suppose there were to be flashed on that screen the things that have occupied the thought cells of our brain. Then there would flash the things that have come to us in the realm of the spirit! Which would be the greater? Self or Christ? Flesh or Spirit? The message of death or the gospel of life? Methinks, perchance, some of us would be a little surprised at how little space God has occupied.

All around us people are dying because they do not know the Truth! O, that they could hear the words, "I am the Truth!" The Truth itself and not merely the Truth imparter! When we know the Truth, He sets us free from self and liberates us from the law of sin and of death. The men of Athens had religion plus and yet they confessed their emptiness when they erected an altar and inscribed upon it, "To the Unknown God." Paul perceived and understood the emptiness of their religion, and preached unto them the power of the Resurrection and the indwelling Christ! He alone can satisfy! So, after 6,000 years of the occupancy of the flesh—6,000 years since the Fall—the Second Adam now comes to take over and in so many lives He finds no room! No room in the inn! No room for the birth of Jesus again within the earthly temples which we are. The Light came unto the darkness and the darkness comprehended it not!

Can He be knocking at the door of our hearts and is the knocking of that nail-pierced hand drowned out by the noises of the demands of self and the impulses of our flesh-life? We may call ourselves rich, but poor are we if all we have accumulated are the things which go with the fleshly man! Even the wisdom that is not the wisdom that is born of above will pass away! Knowledge, if it is not the knowledge of His revealed truth, will not stand in the day of

His appearing! Is not the wisdom of man foolish-
ness with God? It is time we became mature sons of
God. It is time we had a SINGLE EYE toward God.
We cannot come up any other way! It is wholly of
Grace. We cannot DO it, but we can certainly HIN-
DER! He gives us "power to become" and we hinder
God in His purposes in bringing us back into vital
relation with God the Father.

Perhaps we have dealt too much with external
manifestation. We may want to be kind and tender
and gentle and sweet! Now God is the Author of all
these things, but we can also be kind and tender and
gentle and sweet *in the flesh*. Our Father does want
us to manifest these qualities, but the important thing
is that they be the manifestations of His indwelling
and not the product of our own will. That is accepting "the best that we can do" rather than accepting
Him who is our all and in all! There are many seemingly good ways, but there is a way that seemeth
right unto a man, but the end thereof, turns out to
be the way of death. Oh, that we could hear the
Voice behind us saying, "This is the Way; walk ye in
it!" That way is GOD'S WAY. It certainly is not
ours. It is not the way of the flesh. It is the way of
the Spirit. If we walk in the way of His life, we
must, of necessity walk the way of our death. "The
way of the Lord is strength to the upright!" (Proverbs 10:29)

Let us refrain from putting up the barriers of

our Christless selves and our unsanctified reason against the operation of the Divine flow! How foolish will be the wisdom of the worldly wise when the wisdom of the Lord is, at last, made manifest! "The fear of the Lord is the beginning of wisdom: and the knowledge of the Holy is understanding. For by Me thy days shall be multiplied, and the years of thy life shall be increased." (Proverbs 9:10, 11)

CHAPTER VIII

ALL THINGS ARE READY

 *"Come now, and let us reason together, saith the Lord: though your sins be as scarlet, they shall be as white as snow; though they be red like crimson, they shall be as wool. If ye be willing and obedient, ye shall eat the good of the land."* (Isaiah 1:18, 19)

YES, COME NOW, let us reason together! Has your life been one that has had little time for God? That need not be a tragedy! You have led a busy life in the pursuits of the world and there has been so little time for Him! Your circumstances of life have been such that your days have been filled with labor and the cares of this life! That need not be a tragedy! There are many people who have absolutely nothing to do and oft times they are the farthest away from God! They have felt themselves rich and have imagined that they had need of nothing! Their circumstances in life have put them in a position where they have relied upon passing, material, temporal things to supply what they thought were their needs. For so many others, the road has been hard. It has been labor and toil and now such may have come to the consciousness of their need for His indwelling presence. We have often heard it said that if one really wants to get something done, he finds a busy man to do it! The truth we wish to impress is that GOD IS AVAILABLE NOW! People who, of necessity, are occupied with earning the daily bread are often tempted to believe that had they the leisure time of others they could become the recipients of His grace and the objects of its fulfilled promises. There is LIFE FOR A LOOK AT THE CRUCIFIED ONE! There is life and health and strength at this moment for *thee!*

How many times our God has revealed Himself and spoken some flaming message of revealed truth when his children have been, seemingly, preoccupied with other things! David was caring for the sheep in the fields outside Bethlehem of Judea when the call of God, through Samuel, came to him. Samuel himself, as a child, was sleeping when his name was spoken and the voice of God sounded through the temple courts! Joseph was exceeding busy with the routine tasks of his appointed life when God intervened and brought a burning message to his soul. Amos was no prophet; neither was he the son of a prophet. Just a herdsman out in the field! Just a gatherer of sycamore fruit! But then God came to

him and he met the Eternal face to face! Gideon was
a busy man on the threshing floor when the angel of
the Lord appeared to him. Little did he realize the
implications in that call and how the Spirit of the
Lord was to be upon him in the day when the breaking of the pitchers revealed the light which was hidden within! The disciples were all busy men, gather-
ing taxes; fishing in blue Galilee or working in an
apothecary's chamber. They, too, were occupied with
the tasks of this world 'TIL JESUS CAME! But
through them the power of God was to manifest
itself until the course of history would be changed.
They were not to spend their years in vain regrets.
They were to leave their fishing nets and FOLLOW
HIM! When He called them, they were to answer!

And so, beloved, look not regretfully back at
the past and upbraid yourself because of the things
you think you might have done. His grace is not a
reward for your accomplishment; neither is His
healing given as a prize because of longevity of service under His Divine command. Perhaps you have
toiled all night and caught nothing just as the disciples toiled on the rolling waters of Galilee. Perhaps,
you, like they, are coming in with an empty boat.
Yet, in the grey dawn of the early morning, as the
form of the Stranger of Galilee was silhouetted
against the darkness, they heard a welcome invitation, "COME AND DINE!" They were not only to
come to Him, but they were to receive what He had

to give. That is what He wants to do with you. He is not only calling you, but He wants you to come and dine! He wants you to take what He has to give. He has the table spread! He has the bounties there! *Christ has provided!* "But when the morning was now come, Jesus stood on the shore, but the disciples knew not that it was Jesus. Then Jesus saith unto them, Children have ye any meat? They answered Him, No!" They had no meat! It was not long before, in obedience to His command, the 153 fish filled the net and in addition to that, other fish were broiling on the fire for the breakfast His loving hands had prepared.

COME AND DINE

Many of God's dear children have labored hard and toiled all night, only to find in the breaking of the day, as beholding Him, they saw not only the Christ but what the Christ provided for them. No need for it to be an arduous, uphill task! No need for you to try to do over again what He has already done! The provision has been made. Christ's words have been heralded through the ages: "It is finished." And with what gratitude we approach that table, to find that what the Lord has provided completely satisfies! Satisfies more than anything this world can give! Satisfies more than pride and self accomplishment! Satisfies more than the plaudits of people ringing in our ears! The broken cisterns of this world provided no water that would take away the thirst; only Christ can satisfy! And He will satisfy you!

You may live in some remote place where the sound of church bells rarely falls on your ears. You have longed for the voice of some man of God to instruct or to advise; to encourage and comfort and help. But such has been denied you. Hearken! Cannot ye hear the voice of the Lord calling to you, "Behold I stand at the door and knock. If any man hear my voice and open the door, I will come in to him, and will sup with him, and he with Me." Have the doors of your heart been opened recently to bid welcome to the Christ? Have you heard Him say, "What wilt thou that I should do unto thee?" That is just what He is saying. That is what He is calling. That is what He wants to do. He would meet your need. He would give His strength for your weakness. He would impart His fullness for your emptiness. He would let the flow of His resurrection life touch your mortal bodies until disease and sickness and suffering would be past.

Can you not reach out and say, "Lord, just one touch and I will be made whole!" Did the woman who had an issue of blood look to herself or to her past as something essential for the deliverance which the Christ imparted? The burning passion of her heart was, "Jesus is here and if I can only reach Him, I know He will heal me. If I can but touch the hem of His garment, I know I shall be made whole."

Pressing through the throng, she reached out and with the tips of her fingers, contacted the Christ! From Him VIRTUE FLOWED! Virtue sufficient to banish her sickness! Virtue more than enough to meet her every need! Lifted from her despondency; delivered from the slavery of her disease, she gave the glory to the Lord because she knew that her victory was only in the Christ! So it is we should pray, "Cause me to delight to do Thy will, O God! Take from me all that would hinder."

CALLING FOR THEE

Beloved, He is calling for thee! He will never be satisfied until His strength is made perfect in your weakness. We have a BIG GOD! Just as big as our need! He is not only able, but willing to do for us far more abundantly than we are able to ask or think. Have we been talking to Him lately? Have we waited to hear His answer? If we should hear Him speak, the sound of all other voices will fade and we will long for a place of communion daily! All one should want is to walk and talk with Him! He speaks and the sound of His voice is so sweet that the birds hush their singing! Has your heart been open to hear Him who is willing to speak? Have you, in the midst of life's turmoil, and the multitude of your own needs, longed for the touch of the hands which were pierced for you on the Cross of Calvary? He is your healing! He is your strength! He is your wisdom and your sanctification and your righteousness! Christ is your all and in all! He is all you need.

Yes, Lord, "Thy Name is as an ointment poured forth!" (Songs of Solomon 1:3) Thy Name (Thy Nature) is as ointment poured forth! The very Being of Jesus is a healing balm. Yes, beloved, touch Him, and virtue will flow once again from His riven side. He is not a God that is afar off, but is made nigh unto each of us, by His blood.

The desire of His heart is that He would come at our volitional surrender and dwell within continually. "Lead me, O Lord, that I might make straight paths for Thee." Then we shall see that His living presence is something more than the miracle of healing. It is the impartation of His Divine Health! It is the flow of the Resurrection Life through our lives. We shall not only know His *healing power*, but we shall experience His *keeping* power. If He is able to do for us exceeding abundantly more than we can ask or think, is the maintenance of the Divine Life too great a thing to ask? Are not our lives hid with Christ in God? Has unbelief closed the doors through which He would enter to the very heart and center of the entities which we are? Is Jesus a creed or an experience? Divine Health for the body is not beyond the range of possibility for WITH GOD ALL THINGS ARE POSSIBLE.

If we could but give from the depths of our soul, the ABC's—the elementary things—the initial truths

—we would say that JUST WHERE YOU ARE the Lord will meet you! Even for the "toddlers" in Christ—for the ones who know Him the least who, perchance might peruse these pages, we would say, just where you are, and whatever your problem might be, open your heart now to Christ. Let Him in! But some may say, "I do not know how." No, and you never will! But if you are WILLING, that willingness and even faint desire will draw Him into your very presence and He will show you, step by step, just how to come to Him. He will reveal to you how to lay down your burden and believe God. It is not of your effort. It is through the miracle of His grace. He does for us what we can never do for ourselves. Foolish, then, are we to maintain our struggle to attain or to bring about accomplishments. It is the broken and the contrite heart that He will not despise.

THE CONQUEROR

As He comes and reveals His presence and the warm glow of His redeeming love and the miracle-working power of His grace are translated by Him into experience, it will not be hard to draw from Him the things which He imparts. If you do not understand, He does! Lean on Him! Trust Him! Believe Him! Receive Him! And it will not be long before the shadows flee away.

If, on the other hand, you have known Him most of your life and have followed Him for years it would be fair for each one of us to follow the same simple instruction! Come to Jesus—and KEEP COMING! Lay down every burden at His feet—and KEEP TRUSTING HIM! Do not struggle to do it, for all the struggling of a lifetime will not bring it to pass. Let Him do it. He wants to. He is willing. He gave His life so that you might live, and, living, find that He is dwelling in you. If it could be brought about by our own struggles, then there would have been no need for our Substitute to suffer in our stead upon the Cross of Calvary! So draw nigh, in full assurance and make ready your heart. Make ready the heart in simple surrender, that the King of Glory might come in. "Lift up your heads, O ye gates and be ye lifted up ye everlasting doors and the King of glory shall come in. Who is this King of glory? The Lord strong and mighty! The Lord mighty in battle! Lift up your heads, O ye gates, even lift them up ye everlasting doors and the King of glory shall come in. Who is this King of glory. The Lord of hosts, He is the King of glory!" (Ps. 24:7-10)

Never mind the gates of Jerusalem! Put not all your thought upon the doors of the temple. When the glorious day arrives, when He shall triumphantly enter there, He then will see that every provision is made and the promise is absolutely and minutely fulfilled! But open the gates of the temple, WHICH TEMPLE YOU ARE! Open the doors of the heart and LET THE KING OF GLORY IN! Let the

Conqueror come! Let the One who went down into death to bring you Eternal Life enter and dwell within you! Let the One who bore your griefs and sorrows and sicknesses in His own body come within and, having defeated all the enemies of man, He would bring to you the power of His eternal victory! Victory over sin, disease and death! Make straight paths for the King! For He cometh to you!

All things are possible to them that believe! All things are freely given! "He that spared not His own son but delivered Him up for us all, how shall He not, with Him, also, freely give us all things." (Rom. 8:32) All things! No ambiguity there! No limitations on that promise! Whoever you are, it covers your need. Whatever your sickness, it meets it. Whatever your problem, it solves it. Whatever your question, it answers it. ALL THINGS! Freely given to us by God! Come for ALL THINGS ARE NOW READY! "Charge them that are rich in this world that they be not high-minded nor trust in uncertain riches, but in the Living God, who giveth us richly ALL THINGS to enjoy!" (II Timothy 6:17) What a majestic sweep does that glorious promise embrace. All that we have, and all that we are! Nothing is left out! When our loving Lord says, "ALL THINGS," He means ALL THINGS. When the beloved John was on the isle of Patmos and the Lord pulled back the curtains that divide this world He died to redeem from the Father's House of many mansions, one of the last things the Lord revealed to him was the richness of the inheritance of all who will receive the Lord. "He that overcometh shall inherit ALL THINGS, and I will be his God, and he shall be My son." (Rev. 21:7)

ALL THINGS

As man in the initial Fall lost all things, so in the magnitude of the Divine Redemption, ALL THINGS WERE PROMISED TO THE RE- DEEMED SONS OF GOD! "No good thing will He withhold from them that walk uprightly!" O, child of God, how rich you are! Yet without Him, you are miserably poor! O, son of God, how full you are! Yet, unless it is His fullness, how empty and void your heart and life! In ourselves we are NOTHING; but through grace, we have not only been redeemed and cleansed, but have been privileged to become par- takers of His Divine Nature. When we go forth in His Name, it means that we possess HIS NATURE! "According as His divine power hath given unto us ALL THINGS that pertain unto life and godliness, through the knowledge of Him that hath called us to glory and virtue . . ." (II Pet. 1:3)

These, then, are the riches of our inheritance! These, then, are the ALL THINGS which we are privileged to receive in Christ. Call it no longer impossible, for with God all things are possible! Say no longer that it cannot be done, for with Him all

things have already been done! On this foundation
of revealed and impregnable truth, we take our
stand! Then, having done all, we still STAND! But
no longer do we stand in anxiety, but we stand in
faith, BELIEVING! Having no confidence in the
fact of our "standing" but in the One who told us
to stand and in the One who is able to keep us! Having confidence that in His care there will be no cessa-
tion from His providence! Knowing that once His
love imparted has been received there will be no
withdrawing of such love! "Like as a father pitieth
his children, so the Lord pitieth them that fear Him.
He knoweth our frame. He remembereth that we
are dust." (Ps. 103:13) A broken and a contrite
heart He will not despise. He has promised to make
YOU complete in Him, and so He will!

CHAPTER IX

THE FORM OF A MAN!

MARVELOUS in our eyes have been the manifestations of the love and grace of our dear Lord, in touching bodies of so many of His children and raising them up from their sick beds to health. We always have been deeply conscious of the fact that in Divine Healing it is the impartation of His Life, the dissemination of His power, and that without the presence of the Miracle Worker, the miracle could not have been. It is God's purpose, however, in His RE-CREATION to bring forth sons LIKE HIMSELF. God's ultimate in the far-flung reaches of His Redemptive ministry is to bring us into the full possession of everything we gain in Christ. The last enemy that shall be destroyed is Death!

He gives us power to become *sons!* A superficial examination of that statement will not reveal to us the glorious light of His eternal truth in its fullness. His INCREASE is always commensurate with OUR DECREASE. The abundance of His life is predicated upon the willingness of our death. As we allow the more abundant life to manifest itself in us and through us by the recognition of His lovely presence, we are made partakers of the Divine Nature. At first there may be the conflict. Reason may step in and persuade us of the impossibility of such a marvelous transformation. But as self abdicates, a NEW KING IS ON THE THRONE! That King is Christ and the manifestation of His life begins to flow in us and through us until, not only in doctrine, but in actuality, we can say, "For me to live is Christ!"

It is not our life struggling to be like His, but it is the FLOW OF THE LIFE OF CHRIST! We not only become partakers of the Divine Nature, but we become the Divine Nature. We cannot *partake* without *becoming*. And we cannot *become*, without *partaking*. What is the Source of those rivers of Living Water that shall flow out of our innermost being? Do they flow from our depraved natures? Do they flow from self? Are they originated in flesh? Do they find their source in human reason or in the manifestation and exercise of our wills? Everything about *us* is corrupt. Our very bodies groan and suffer with their unspeakable corruption! Our natures are depraved. Our thoughts are unclean, and search where you will, there is no little tributary of purity to be found anywhere within the natural man. Yet, from us, there can flow RIVERS OF LIVING WATER! These life-giving streams are not fed by tributaries of reason nor of intellect nor of will. They spring from the ARTESIAN WELLS OF THE DIVINE LIFE which is operating within. Everywhere they go, as they flow from beneath the throne of our spirits, they bring healing and salvation; life and truth, and everything they touch is changed from glory to glory! No part of the entity which we are can be hidden from their purifying, sanctifying flow! What a world of difference there is between this New Creation life in Christ Jesus and the ceaseless struggle of well-meaning people to live Christian lives, and by trying to do good and to be good, make Heaven their home at last!

When Jesus was here among men, He was the WORD MADE FLESH! He was the Virgin-born, Son of God, incarnate in a body made like unto the form of a man, for He took upon Himself the form of a man and dwelt among us. But the Holy Spirit turns the light of revelation upon the Entity Who dwelt within that external form of flesh. We are not our bodies; they are merely the habitations in which *we* dwell. They are the mediums through which we are able to express ourselves. As the body is more than meat or raiment; so the real man is more than the body!

WHO HE WAS

When we look at the face of a watch, we are able to tell the time; but a watch is something more than face and hands and printed figures! Inside there is a mechanism and every part must move in perfect obedience and correlation with every other part. The hands and face of the watch are important, but they are merely the index of the mechanism which works within. The Scribes and Pharisees could see what Jesus did but they could not see Who He was. Their eyes were blinded to the identity of the inner mechanism. There in the form of a human body dwelt the God-head! There was GOD HIMSELF, manifesting Himself through an outer covering of flesh. He clothed Himself upon with humanity. Jesus Himself said, "The works I do I do not of Myself and the words I speak I speak not of Myself." (John 14:10, 11) There is nothing ambiguous about that statement. It is pungent with truth divine. "He that hath seen Me hath seen the Father!"

The difficulty was that many people could look at Him and yet not see Him. They saw what He did but they did not see Him. They heard what He said, but they could not hear Him. They had eyes but they were blind. They had ears but they were deaf. His life was the manifestation of the Divine Life, operating in and through a human form. He is *our* life and we supply the FORM OF A MAN, even as Christ supplied the form of a Man in which the Father dwelt! When do we see the FORM OF THE FOURTH? "Lo, I see four men loose, walking in the midst of the fire, and they have no hurt; and THE FORM OF THE FOURTH IS LIKE THE SON

OF GOD!" (Daniel 3:25) It is when we see the form of the three (the triune man: body, soul and spirit) *changed*, like unto His glorious Being! It is then that we see the form of the Fourth, which is the Christ! Even as the Living Creatures of Ezekiel, "they had the LIKENESS of a man!" (Ezekiel 1:5)

But our blessed Lord did not stop there! In the very next verse, the 12th, He said, "Verily, verily, I say unto you, He that believeth on Me, the works that I do shall he do also; and greater works than these shall he do; because I go unto my Father." This scripture declares that the works which Jesus did were going to be duplicated by the disciples who would leave all to follow Him. Now if the works He did were not His own but were the works of the Father and those works were going to be duplicated in us, would we have the power apart from the Father's indwelling presence to perform such works? If the life that Jesus lived was a manifestation of the Divine Life and His promise was that we were to have the same identical Waters of Life flowing through us, would they originate in God in the life of Christ and originate, apart from God, in us? God forbid!

Did He not say to His disciples, "Yet a little while, and the world seeth Me no more; but ye see Me: because I live, ye shall live also. At that day ye shall know that I am in my Father, and ye in Me, and I in you." (John 14:19, 20) Let the full impact of that glorious declaration resound through the corridors of your being until the magnitude of its implications overwhelms you! We were to be partakers of the CHRIST-LIFE! There was to be no difference. As God once manifested Himself in the Son of God, so He was going to manifest Himself in the sons of God. It was not to be human life, transformed and made like His; it was to be the Divine Life flowing through vessels of clay and so permeating them that they would become partakers of the Divine Nature.

In other words, there was to be no difference between the spirit which was in the Christ and the spirit which was in us! The burning object of this writing is to bring into vital union with the quickening power of God those who have been limited in such contact by the boundaries of denomination-alized theologies; by self-will, or by limited vision and desire. We became separated from the life of God, through the Fall, and have remained so separated because of our insistence on living in the fallen state. But it is now God's plan that His life be restored to the sons of men!

TO KNOW HIM

There is within each one of us a cavity—an empty place—of which even sinful men are conscious. Particularly is this emphasized in the lives of those who have given themselves to Him, and yet who have not completely surrendered. There is the

constant pull of the Spirit. There is an increasing
hunger and desire. Such was epitomized in the cry
of the apostle, "O, that I might know Him and the
power of His Resurrection." It was not an understanding of some creedal truth for which he craved.
It was not only to be led by the Spirit into the concepts of eternal verities which were only made possible by the illuminating, revealing power of the Spirit.
It was that he might come into DIRECT, VITAL
UNION WITH THE CHRIST! That as the Father
and the Son were one, so that we, too, might become
ONE, even as Jesus had prayed when He poured out
His heart in that prayer which embraced the reasons
why He came and the desires of His divine heart!

It is in this age, the age of Laodicea, that our Lord
is standing at the door of human hearts, knocking
with His nail-pierced hands, "Behold I stand at the
door and knock. If any man hear My voice, and
open the door, I will come in to him, and will sup
with him, and he with Me." (Rev. 3:20) How er-
roneously have we applied this text in our dealing
with sinful man. It is at the door of *His Church*
Christ is standing. So many worship Him, whom they
do not, experimentally, know. They look on the ex-
terior for the manifestation of His presence, and sit
and sigh for the day in which He shall appear. But to
others, He has already come within! His Kingdom
has been established; His throne has been set up. He
lives within our hearts! He rules within the confines

of our natures. The day will come, undoubtedly, when He shall appear again in clouds! But I do not want to be among that number who are only looking, outwardly, for the sign of His coming in the sky. I would rather belong to that number who would say, "Farewell" to the sordid, morbid things of our sinful selves, and open the door of the being to His glorious indwelling and testify, "He lives—He lives—He lives within my heart!"

BEING BECOME

Thus it is that God wants to deal with humanity. It is more than singing hymns. It is more than prayer. It is BEING BECOME! It is the recognition of His Life within. It is not asking for it, only, it is experiencing it! It is becoming it. Then, as has been said, in part, "If we think of prayer as the breath in our lungs and the blood in our veins, we think of it rightly." For this cause are we being recreated, that we might become the manifestations of the presence of God in the flesh. "Know ye not that your bodies are the temples of the Living God?" Are we not being builded together, stone upon stone, for a habitation of God in the Spirit? Is not this Divine indwelling the goal of every man who determines, by God's grace, to walk no longer after the flesh, but after the Spirit? Then the triumphant cry rings out! A cry that is foolishness to men, but marvelous to the redeemed and the angels; "It is no longer I, but Christ, who dwelleth in me."

Now, this "being become" is progressive. It is not imparted in a moment. It is not attained in an instant nor in a life-time. The truth is that we never attain; we rather RECEIVE! We cannot earn the gift of His Life; neither can anything we can do create it within ourselves. He brings it. He is it! It is when we LET HIM live in us and through us that the manifestation of that life begins to assert itself. The ministry of the perpetuation of it and the development of it is His and His alone! We must let go— and let God! In all our ways, we must acknowledge Him, and then He will direct our paths. If we keep our lives, we shall lose them. If we lose our life, for His sake, we shall find it. That is it! For His sake! That He might be in our hearts. For His Name's sake —and that means HIS NATURE'S SAKE!

This can bring us to no other place than radiant health for body and for soul and for spirit. As there is no sin in His nature, there can be no sickness either. *That is the ultimate!* That is the place to which He is bringing His children. He was wounded for our transgression and because of His sacrificial death on the Cross of Calvary, we can enter into the fullness of the possession of His eternal life. The glorious economy of SUBSTITUTION does not fall down in the slightest degree; neither does His vicarious suffering disintegrate at any part. It was FINISHED. It is COMPLETE. It was perfected on Calvary and Jesus meant what He said when He cried out from the Cross, "It is finished." He took our sorrows. He bore our griefs. He carried our infirmities. He took all our pains. He bore them in His own Body to the tree. He even took our death and, substitutionally, atoned for the penalty of our transgression when He hung His head and died, as the sun went down on Calvary.

HIS VICTORY

He entered into death and overcame it. He went into the grave and from it He arose triumphantly and victoriously! The strongest of the satanic forces came to grips with Him, and He conquered them all! He conquered them every one! He came in triumph from the tomb—robed in glory—and clothed with His own Resurrection life. Through the long corridors of the ages, in triumph, His voice has cried, "Because I live, ye shall live also!" He came that we might have life and that we might have it more abundantly! It is not His plan that we put our necks under the yoke of an Adamic creation and believe that it is the purpose of our Heavenly Father to keep us there! There is relief and comfort in the shadow of the Rock in a weary land. There is a Shelter in time of storm. There is deliverance from habit. There is emancipation from sin. There is freedom from disease. Not from without! But from the life that wells up and springs up within. Healing rays of the Sun of righteousness are not only going to come up over the mountains of Time, in some wonderful Tomorrow, as so many of us dream, but they will arise TODAY, over the surrendered spirits of men who have yielded their all to follow in the way that He would lead. It is health for body and for soul and for spirit. It is life—His life! Radiant and glorious and overcoming! The waters that at first were to the ankles have become WATERS TO SWIM IN!

The oceans of His love bear us up as the billows of glory and praise roll around on every hand and side. The boat does not carry the ocean, but the ocean carries the boat. The man or woman who, in self, is always striving to attain is like the traveler who leaves New York for Europe and insists on getting out and swimming and pushing the boat ahead. How hopeless the effort. How futile the task. Know we not that He will CARRY US THROUGH? All He asks is that we leave the old shores and embark for the new. All He wants is that we surrender completely unto Him. "To as many as receive Him to them gave He power to become sons..." And the "power to become" is in the recognition of the truth that in ourselves we can never become—only as He becomes in us! Then the billows bear us over. Then, like the ark, we sail away. The waters of judgment do not enfold us. We ride above them. God would not let man shut the door. He did that Himself. He would not give him a wheel or a prow with which to guide the boat. It must be guided entirely by the Lord!

HID WITH CHRIST

Can the human mind conceive of a greater privilege or the human spirit be lost in contemplation of an experience more sublime? Know ye not that our lives are hid with Christ in God? He died and I died too. He went into the grave and I went with Him there. He rose in triumph and I rose with Him. He ascended and so did I. Yes, and so did you! And so did all the children of Redemption who will enter into this glorious oneness with their Lord! What a world of difference there is between trying to live the Christian life and LETTING the Christ of Eternal Life dwell in us.

And so, He is leading His dear children along! The time is not far off when another line will be added to the triumphant song, "So when this corruptible shall have put on incorruption, and this mortal shall have put on immortality, then shall be brought to pass the saying that is written, Death is swallowed up in victory. O death, where is thy sting? O grave, where is thy victory? The sting of death is sin; and the strength of sin is the law. But thanks be to God, which giveth us the victory through our Lord Jesus Christ." (I Cor. 15:54-57)

So we can say of a glorious truth that for me to live is Christ and to die is gain! This incorruptible life is not only to be found after one is dead and buried. But it is included in the "being become..." in the recreation of the New Creation. It is there that we are made back into His Image. Well might the exultant spirit cry, "Emmanuel! Emmanuel!"— God with us! God with us!

Beloved, this is our Land of Promise. This is Beulah Land and Beulah means "married." Married to Christ! Separted from the world and the flesh and made ALIVE UNTO GOD! Entering into the richness and the fullness of His life and experiencing and enjoying the flow of the Divine Nature and all of the victory that He purchased for us on Calvary. We are standing today at the gates of our Promised Land. Let us not be like the ones of old, who at Kadesh-Barnea listened to the voices of reason and turned back into the wilderness! What if they were the majority? Has the majority always been right? In my heart, I can hear the Master speak, "Fear not, LITTLE FLOCK, it is your Father's good pleasure to give you the Kingdom." Not the "great flock" but the "little flock". Not the masses, but the chosen few. Not the preponderance of opinion but the surrendered and yielded minority. To them, He will give the Kingdom and if they would know the glory of the reigning in the Kingdom without, they must first experience the beauty of His reign in the Kingdom within.

OUR PROMISED LAND

And when at last we enter into our Canaan; when we feel beneath the souls of our feet the hills and vales of the Land of Promise, we stand secure in Him! Whose power is it that brought us across the Jordan? By Whose power and at Whose Word did the walls of Jericho fall? Who is the conqueror of the giants? Who is it unfolds the portals of the city and opens the gate-ways to the vales where the grapes of Eschol grow? Was it *their* marching? Was it the power of *their* might? Was it what *they* did? Every pulsating sentence of the typical Record throbs with the revelation of the Divine truth! He, who even now is the Author and Finisher of our faith, was the One who pushed the walls of Jericho down. He spoke and the waters divided. He came at the time of the extremity of Joshua's judgment and outlined the plan by which they would be more than conquerors. It was His power and His alone. And so, today, the flesh and our human natures must run up the flag of unconditional surrender to our eternal Christ! All they had to do in those days of old was to walk in obedience and that is just exactly what we have to do today. Not only, when traveling days are over shall we be able to sing, "For Thine is the Kingdom and the Power and the Glory!" But we should, of a truth, be able to sing it now. His will is being done in the earth, which we are, and in us, dear Lord, Thine is the Kingdom—and Thine is the power—and Thine is the glory! The work is Thine! The life is Thine! The nature is Thine! The flow of the rivers from beneath the Throne of the surrendered heart are the waters of Thine own Resurrection life and whatsoever those waters touch is healed.

Open the gates of the temple! Let the King of glory in! Open the gates of the temple! The temple which we are! And let us make our very spirits a habitation for the dwelling of the Eternal God! Then the weary spirit is refreshed by the rivers of His grace. His Love Divine, all loves excelling begins to permeate every fibre of our beings. Not a love *like* His—but His Divine Love! The battle is over and the victory is won! The troubled, burdened heart knows the beauty of His peace! It does not rest quiescent in contemplation of what He will do, but it sinks back in the Everlasting Arms and praises Him for what He is. The peace we enjoy is not ours. It is His. And with what rapturous joy the ransomed spirit sings the story of the New Creation Life! It is not the joy of being entertained by the frivolities of a sinful world. It is the joy that the angels experience when they sing around the Throne or tune their harps by the glassy sea.

This is the genius of our Christ! This is the Story of Redemption. The mind cannot comprehend it and only the redeemed and surrendered heart can begin to understand it; but praise His Name, we are being so changed in the inner man—changed by His Spirit, as we behold His image as in a glass, from glory unto glory, that it is no wonder that when at last we awaken, it will be in His Likeness. Rivers of

Salvation! Rivers of Healing! Rivers of Victory and
of Glory! Rivers of Triumph over Death! Rivers—
not of death waters—but of Living Waters, spring-
ing up and flowing out unto Life Eternal.

CHAPTER X

THE REPAIRER OF THE BREACH!

"... and thou shalt be called the repairer of the breach; the restorer of paths to dwell in." (Is. 58:12)
"Now this I say, brethren, that flesh and blood cannot inherit the Kingdom of God; neither doth corruption inherit incorruption." (I Cor. 15:50)

WE ARE COMING TO THE SOVEREIGN RULE OF GOD, both in the earth which we *are*, and in the outer earth, in which dwelleth the nations! The outer is a reflex of the inner and there is a distinct parallel between the things which shall happen without and the things which happen within! As in the outer world, kings and princes and potentates will, ultimately, give way to the Rule of Christ and lay their crowns at His feet, so in the inner there must be the capitulation and surrender of all that we have and all that we are to the RULE OF THE LORD! We cannot have a duality of Headship. No man can serve two masters! The Sovereign Lord

must exercise His sovereign rule within as, ultimately, He will exercise that sovereign rule without!

God has given His children their EVICTION
NOTICES! As we vacate, He comes in! It is because
we, ourselves, have been ruling and reigning in our
tenancy that the building which we are is in such sad
need of repair. Repairs of body, of soul and of spirit!
He is revealing to us the fact that we are incapable
of repairing ourselves in any department of our lives.
As we move out, HE MOVES IN! Now, one that
vacates is not concerned with the repairs, for that is
the problem for the new owner. He comes in to do
what we could never do! He who said, "Let there
be . . ." in the beginning can again utter His man-
date, "Let there be . . ." and the earth which we are
becomes obedient to His Voice. As He comes to
dwell within we find that He is the REPAIRER OF
THE BREACH and the restorer of paths to dwell in.
He is our restoration! The fact of our surrender and
capitulation means the assumption of His rule and,
then, "for me to live is CHRIST" becomes, in actuality, our testimony and our experience. No longer
do we have to struggle with the business of repairing.
Our ransomed spirits delight in HIS AUTHORITY!
Every part of the nature responds to His leadership.
It is not of mind nor of understanding, for His ways
are past finding out. But that does not detract from
the reality and the majesty and power of His leading.
Thus for body, soul and spirit, He becomes the re-

pairer of the breach, and the restorer of paths to dwell in.

The statesmen of the world are sitting at so-called peacetables trying to fix international boundary lines and decide upon the confines of the nations. In Psalm 24:1 it says, "The earth is the LORD'S and the fullness thereof; the world and they that dwell therein!" He has declared, "The meek shall inherit the earth!" The nations are "squatting," so to speak, on borrowed ground! Their corrupt tenancy has fallen to pieces and is distintegrating because they have not allowed the rightful Owner to have any voice in the government. They have substituted their ways for His ways. They have pushed aside His thoughts and have chosen their own. But He has not abandoned this iniquitous earth for it is His treasured possession! It is His footstool! It belongs to Him! And the day is very near when He is coming to claim His ownership and when He, with His sovereign rule moves in to the Throne of Authority, man in his Adamic rule will have to move out.

POSSESS YE

Now, we have been "squatters" so to speak in this earth, which *we* are. We do not belong to ourselves. How can we belong to ourselves when we have been redeemed and purchased with so great a price? We have been bought with that price and we are not our own. That price is the Blood that He shed on

Calvary to redeem us from the possession of the enemy and to buy us back as His purchased possession. And He is coming to take over that possession! We have no right, reigning and ruling within ourselves! We must abdicate. He must be seated upon the throne of the heart and until He does take His seat there, we shall never be in full possession of our inheritance. Possess ye your vessels! But this cannot be done until the Possessor possesses!

We have been used to ruling by reason. We have been utilizing the ways that seem right to a man, forgetting, meanwhile that such roads lead to death. There is no road but the "death road" upon which a human can travel, for the only life we are privileged to contact is CHRIST! So the broken entity called self, with all its corruption of body, soul and spirit, MUST MOVE OUT! The true Possessor of the earth, which we are, is asking that we let Him move in. Then, when His sovereignty is experienced, health supersedes disease; strength banishes weakness and death gives way to life! He Himself becomes our life!

Paul, the apostle, surrendered to the Headship of Christ! That is why he was able to tell the Galatians, "I am crucified with Christ; nevertheless I live—yet not I—but Christ liveth in me and the life which I now live in the flesh I live by the faith of the Son of God who loved me and gave Himself for me." (Gal. 2:20) In other words, in that fleshly tabernacle in which once dwelt Saul of Tarsus, there now was DWELLING THE CHRIST! The faith within him was not his belief in Christ, but the FAITH WHICH CHRIST IMPARTED TO HIM. The life he was living was not his own. It was the life of Christ proving sufficient for every emergency and vitalizing and strengthening him in every time of need. Christ had a right to that body! It was His by virtue of His redeeming sacrifice on Calvary's cross! He died Saul's death that Paul might become the possessor of His Resurrection life! Paul's constant testimony was, "It is no longer I—but Christ—who dwelleth in me." It was HIS life; HIS strength; HIS presence; HIS power; HIS love shed abroad in the heart. It was the peace which Christ imparted. Paul had moved out and Christ had moved in! The repair work was not any longer the struggle of Paul; but rather the efficacious ministry of Christ, permeating His reclaimed possession!

If, then, Christ is living within, what are we doing? What can we do? Why should we try to do anything but ALLOW HIM to rule and reign and have His complete and perfect way with us? What right have we to put our puny judgments up against the flow of His Spirit or allow the craftiness of our own minds to impede the inward and the outward manifestation of the life of God Himself! For us, then, to live is Christ and to die is gain. Our testimony before men and the angels is, "Christ in me, the hope of glory!" But no man can serve two masters. We must move out if He moves in!

GOD'S MAN

In the first world war, history records that General Allenby entered Jerusalem without the firing of a shot! There is no doubt it was in fulfillment of God's prophetic Word. The Arabs called him, "God's man," for his name sounded very much like "Allah" —God; and "bey"—a nobleman. As the General marched in through the Damascus gate, the Moslems left by the gate on the other side of the city. Now the city was still there. The streets were just the same and the buildings had not been transformed. The difference was in the *ownership!* The Moslems moved out and Allenby moved in! Then it was that Allenby began the restoration of the broken places. He brought order out of chaos! He brought government out of anarchy! So as God's Man, who is Christ, comes into our city, through the front door, the "I" life flees out of the back and His rule is established over the city which we are! He begins to reign within! Self is uncovered and carried away! Then the new Owner begins making the necessary repairs. He does it! It is His ministry. The ALL THINGS are only done THROUGH CHRIST! Is power needed to repair the waste places? It is His power. Is health needed to supplant the suffering and the pain? It is His health. As to the woman who had an issue of blood, virtue flowed out from Him, so in the manifestation of His rule in the earth, which we are, virtue is flowing out from His presence and permeating every part of our beings, the earth, which we are, body, soul and spirit!

"When ye therefore shall see the abomination of desolation, spoken of by Daniel the prophet, stand in the holy place, (whoso readeth, let him understand:)" (Matt. 24:15) We find that which maketh desolate taking up its abode within our temples! We find it in the holy place. We find it in its manifestation of its rule in the earth, making the nations desolate. But wherever you discover it, it is the same. It is the "I" life—the self-rule—the headship of man, rather than the RULE OF CHRIST! It is the mind which is in our depraved beings instead of the mind which is in Christ Jesus our Lord. It is the authority of self instead of the authority of God. No matter where you discover it, in the earth as a whole, or in the life in the entities which we are, it is the "I" life and it brings nothing but disaster and disease and suffering and death! It makes desolate everything which it touches. This apostate world, having come to the end of the rule of man, and standing on the very brink of its complete and cataclysmic collapse is soon to lose its own headship before the sovereign rule of the Christ of God!

So, the earth, which we are must lose its own Adamic headship as the King comes whose right it is

to reign. What victory there is when He becomes the
King of our lives! What responsibility is lifted from
our shoulders! We have tried to run things and have
failed, and now He says, "Turn over the reins of
government to Me!" In all your ways acknowledge
Him and He will direct your paths! We begin to
taste the millennial glories within before ever they
are experienced without! We are raptured in Spirit
while waiting for rapture. We do not spend
all our time contemplating a coming future Kingdom without, because, in the meanwhile, we are enjoying the glorious rule of Christ as He reigns in the
Kingdom within.

NOT TOO BIG FOR HIM

When we look at our problems in the flesh, we
cry, "O, this is too big for me!" But we hear His
sweet voice, "It is not too big for ME!" We wrestle
with questions and never find an answer. Then He
takes absolute charge and He begins to answer while
we are yet calling. We wrestle with our problems
and they grow so big that they "get us down." Then,
when we allow Him to rule and reign within, He
picks us up and lifts us with our problems, too, and
we find that they are gone in the light of the revelation of the truth which He is! We find we cannot
live our lives. Of course, we can't! But He can! He
wants to! That is LIVING BY FAITH! That is
living by His Faith. That is not choosing our own
spot, or going where we want to go, and then decide

on doing nothing and call it "living by faith." That is presumption! When the self-life capitulates to God, we find ourselves where God places us and then just LIVE! Live by the faith of the Son of God! Live by the power that is not our own. Drink from the inexhaustible streams of His never-ending supply! Feed upon the Bread which He is! Assimilate His very nature! Refuse to look at flesh and henceforth know no man after the flesh! Rather, SEE CHRIST! And beholding His Glory, we become changed from glory to glory as daily we are made partakers of the Divine Nature. It is not struggling to become "like Him," something that depraved and fallen flesh can never do, but rather LET HIM MOVE IN, as we move out and allow the rule of His Life to operate within.

That was the Divine Pattern. In His earthly ministry, Jesus said He lived by the Father. The words He said and the works He did were not His. They were the Father's. He was in the Father and the Father was in Him! Then He directly prayed that His redeemed children might enjoy an identical experience. As He was animated and moved and lived the embodiment of the Father's will, so we were to be indwelt by Him and we were to become HIS WILL! Not merely do His will; but BECOME it! He would have us live BY THE FAITH OF THE SON OF GOD who gave Himself for us and now would give Himself TO US!

Christ is our BUYER-BACK! God wants us to live on that plane where we do not possess anything.

> *"Nought that I have I call my own,*
> *I owe it to the Giver."*

Everything that we had was fleshly and depraved. We are willing to be dispossessed in order that we might be POSSESSED BY THE POSSESSOR! Then we become "caretakers" on His properties. As caretakers we function. What He imparts, we enjoy. What He gives we utilize. How blessed and sweet this ministry of His Divine indwelling and how blessed the rest for those of His children who come to the realization that when He said, "It is finished," on Calvary, He meant just what He said. It was finished! Everything was accomplished there. There is nothing we can add to it and, certainly, we would never want to take away!

OUR VICTORY

This is peace! This is victory! When the government is turned over, there is no worry. When He becomes Governor, He begins to govern us and all of our affairs. Not theoretically—but actually! Not doctrinely—but experimentally! It is no longer living *a* life, but it is living *His* life, because He Himself is living His life in us. In our bewilderments and problems, God offers us a window opened in heaven and as we enter this, we find it is a life of faith! It is the Way to Life!

In the typical days of the old testament whenever the nation came to the end of itself and was willing to turn the matter over to the Lord, He always took charge and brought His Victory out of their defeat. As long as they struggled to do it, He often let them try. Then, when they came to the confession of their own helplessness, they turned to Him, and He did FOR them and IN them what they could never do for themselves. If that was true in Law, how great are our privileges in this glorious dispensation of Grace! He does not ask us to live our lives; He wants to live them for us! He does not want us to go unless He sends us. He does not ask us to do, unless He does it! The Amalekites and the Jebusites and the Hittites were all phases of the "I" life and they must be overcome and cast out before, in these days of grace, we can enter into the Land of His Promise!

When we recognize the truth that the earth, which we are, is the Lord's and the fullness thereof and the entire earth, body, soul and spirit is turned over to Him, HE CARES FOR IT! He repairs it! He heals it! He breathes His life into it. He imparts His strength. We receive the mind which was also in Christ Jesus our Lord. That is the only mind which is capable of spiritual understanding. Spiritual things are spiritually discerned.

It is then that GOD CAUSES! He causes us to
inherit! He causes us to step out of the way with
our human thoughts and our vain imaginations and
unsanctified reason and allow the FLOW of His Divine presence. The manifestation of His love will flow
through unhindered and unhampered and unchal-
lenged! Nothing can withstand the progression
of that Divine flow. Even Egypt will serve us then!
How much richer this is than struggling to be a
Christian! What paupers we are when we insist upon
utilizing the tools of our own depravity! SLAY
UTTERLY! SLAY until there is no more lowing of
the oxen and bleating of the sheep! Never mind what
reason and human understanding would do about
sacrificial offerings! OBEDIENCE IS BETTER
THAN SACRIFICE and to hearken than the fat of
rams! Surrender entirely and give it over to Him.

HIS RESPONSIBILITY

Then when it is His, it is His responsibility! Peter
realized that when he went to sleep, when he was
incarcerated in prison for the sake of the Lord. He
knew he could not do it but his Lord could! It was
when Peter DID NOTHING that God did EVERY-
THING! Who opened the doors without the hand-
ling of human fingers? Whose power gently woke
him from his rest and sleep, meanwhile keeping his
adversaries insensible to what was going on? That
is what is happening today. God is leading His chil-

dren out of the prison-house in the midst of men
who sleep! They do not see what is going on! They
do not know the hour of this Liberation! We cease
from our labors as Christ ceased from His! Our
very lives become His responsibility. We cannot do it.
But He can! Then when we do not try to do it, He
does!

When Peter and John, with their hearts aflame
from the infilling of the Holy Spirit on the Day of
Pentecost met the man at the Beautiful Gate of the
temple, healing was brought to that man just as if
Christ were there in physical form and presence.
There was no difference. The blind, unbelieving
world around them could not see the Christ and
they fastened their eyes on THEM. How quickly did
those disciples dispel that error. In plain language
they said, "We did not do it, but the Christ ye put
to death was the One who accomplished this miracle."
It was done in the NAME OF JESUS and that means
it was done in the NATURE OF JESUS! It was
done by the power of the indwelling Presence!

Our eviction notices are being sent from Him,
that we vacate, for He is coming in to rule and to
reign. So many of His dear children are spending a
great deal of time, in these closing hours, looking at the external instead of the internal. Every
new leader who comes across the horizon is pro-
claimed an antichrist. They concern themselves with
geographical boundaries and look for signs here and

there. Of what use is all this unless we see the SIGNS WITHIN! It is far more important that we behold the abomination of desolation which is set up in the temple which we are, and that abomination of desolation is the SELF LIFE, than it is that we behold it, only, in the external! Our Father will take care of that when the time comes. The rule without is His business, but it is our business to crown Him within, King of our lives and Lord of all that we are and all that we have, body, soul and spirit.

So here we are! Turning the rulership of this Kingdom (which we are) over to the rightful Ruler, and we are evicted. We relinquish the authority that we thought we had. The government is upon His shoulders and in the earth which we are His will is being done! Then we do not have to wait until some future day to praise Him in the words, "For Thine is the Kingdom and the power and the glory—in the earth which we are—forever and forever!"

CHAPTER XI

INHERIT THE EARTH

"Behold how good and how pleasant it is for brethren to dwell together in unity!" (Ps. 133:1)

NOT ONLY UNITY with each other, but in complete and perfect harmony with the Father, Son and Holy Spirit! "It is like the precious ointment upon the head, that ran down upon the beard, even Aaron's beard: that went down to the skirts of his garments." This ointment covered Aaron completely, from the head to the feet. It covered his garments! How typical it is of that complete and perfect redemptive covering which is the heritage of those who are sons of God and determined to walk in harmony and in unity with Him!

This, of necessity, demands the surrender of the self life. It is only that, if in ALL our ways we acknowledge Him, He has promised to direct our paths! The intermittent leadership is not pleasing to Him, for He would have us come into unity with Himself that

[145]

we, ourselves, would become the living embodiments and expressions of His divine will. He would speak through our lips. He would so live within us, preparing us for that glorious Day, when the pitchers at last will be broken and the manifestation of the Light will shine forth! It will be His Light! His Life! His Presence! His Power! And He Himself will be the Glory which shall, ultimately, be revealed in us!

Now, God is coming in discipline and training in His sons! Always He has had a PERIOD OF PREPARATION for His chosen and anointed people.. Such training and discipline is not always along the paths of our own desires, for whom the Lord loveth, He chasteneth and the heart in which He would dwell is called to obedience, by the things which we must suffer. This discipline and training is not with regard to our salvation which is already firmly established. Our salvation is in the fact that He died for us on Calvary's tree, vicariously and substitutionally taking our transgressions and our iniquities and giving to us His own Holiness and Pardon and Righteousness! There is LIFE FOR A LOOK AT THE CRUCIFIED ONE! And without the Crucified and Resurrected One, we could never be the possesors of His Eternal Life. The discipline and training is in preparation for the *heirs* who are receiving the inheritance and who have been made joint-heirs with Jesus Christ to all of the fullness of the Godhead!

God is training His children! He is preparing the
overcomers for the Throne! His ways are always the
right ways, even though, temporarily, we may not
understand them. His thoughts are not our thoughts!
How precious His leading. As the heavens are higher
than the earth, so are the ways and the thoughts of
God higher than ours. If, perchance, because of our
misinterpretation or misunderstanding, we would
blunder along some path that seems right to us, disciplinary measures are necessary to bring us back
into the PATH OF HIS CHOOSING! Sometimes
this is the road of suffering. From that road we learn
OBEDIENCE, even as our Lord learned obedience by
the things which He suffered.

Human nature is so constructed that it always
wants its own way. It appeals to reason, and receives
from that faculty acquiesence and encouragement to
follow along those paths that seem to be right. We
may not know, but God does, that the end of such
paths leads to *death*. They may seem to be right; but
they are not right. If we are to REIGN WITH
HIM, we must also SUFFER WITH HIM! We must
suffer those things God puts upon us not as punitive
measures, but as remedial. He wants to bring us to
the place of a *surrendered sonship* where a life is completely and wholly directed by Him. The human nature must be supplanted by the Divine Nature, and
as we partake of it, we are changed from glory to
glory and the transformation is so complete and far-

reaching that the Scriptures tell us we can come to
the PERFECT MAN, (*MATURE*) to the fullness
of the stature of Christ! This great goal is not attained by traveling the sentimental pathways of our
own desires, but by being made obedient to the will
and purpose of our Father.

> *"In shady green pastures, so rich and so sweet,*
> *God leads His dear children along!*
> *Where the waters' cool flow bathes the weary*
>   *one's feet,*
> *God leads His dear children along!*
> *Some through the waters; some through the*
>   *flood,*
> *Some through the fires, but all through the*
>   *Blood!*
> *Some through great trials, but God gives a*
>   *song,*
> *In the night seasons and all the day long!"*

THE PRESENCE

It was in the fiery furnace that the form of the
Fourth was seen, walking with the obedient children
and robbing the very fire itself of its power to do
them harm! Would not flesh cringe at the prospect
of a fire? Would not human nature say that it was
cruel for God to allow His children to get into such
a predicament as that? Would not reason say that it
would be more sensible for them to take the easy
way out? The three Hebrew children were typical

of the whole man: body, soul and spirit. They were not disobedient unto the Heavenly vision, but they purposed to be obedient to Him! He was visible in the fire! That is where we, oftimes, see Him, too! He is with us there!

We may feel that when we have our way in life, we have won the victory! But really we have suffered defeat. We get what we wanted in the way we wanted it, but God would have us receive what we need in the way we need it! The obedient son will rejoice in the Lord, no matter what way or in what ever path our Father chooses. We will walk into the fire unafraid; for God is with us! We will take every chastisement and every testing as from the Lord and, because of this, we are able to rejoice in our trials and glory in our infirmities! These light afflictions are working out for us a far more exceeding and eternal weight of glory,

The King of kings is establishing a government that will not only embrace the earth, but the far flung reaches of the universe! His glory shall be revealed in His children! HE IS PREPARING THEM! He is getting them ready! So He is instructing His sons! He is putting us through the system of discipline today, that we may be qualified by His power for the riches of our inheritance tomorrow! If they are to govern, they must first be governed! Before we can be "more than conquerors" we must first be conquered!

HAVE THINE OWN WAY

We have prayed, "Have Thine own way, Lord!"
and even as we prayed have kept an eye on some
path of our own desire! The thing we desire may be
pleasing to the Lord, yet we should be so surrendered
that we are willing to receive it His way. It was all
right for David to bring back the Ark of the Covenant. God wanted it back! It was not the desire
of the Lord that it remain in the hand of the enemy.
But it was to rest again in the temple at Shiloh, and
David knew well that such was God's purpose and
plan. But when he inquired of the Lord as to whether
or not he should go up, the Lord said, "Thou shalt
not go up." David wanted to do God's will in *his
way*. God wanted David to do His will in God's way.
It was not with an army, but with the sound of
a-going in the top of the mulberry trees, that the
victory was to come. The victory was not won on
the battle-field; but it was won when David decided
to obey God.

The world is filled with a thousand and one plans
for bringing back the Ark. Worldly rulers and
authorities are trying to manufacture a synthetic
millennium and the sounds of their dismal failure
are heard on every hand and side. Religious people
everywhere are indulging in sentimentalities in their
vain attempts to bring about the world peace. How
miserably they fail! There is a little minority who
have opened their ears and their lives to the Presence

and the Voice of the Lord. To them, He has been revealing His secrets! They know how it will come! The Word has been unfolded; the Living Word has made the written Word plain! By a miracle of grace, He is indwelling those who have been willing to make the surrender and He is training them in the grace of obedience. He is taking them through fiery furnaces and through paths of which they have never dreamed, but in all their chastening they are conscious of the Divine Love and rejoice in the Divine Presence.

Self must go! Their desires must be laid at His blessed feet in order that the desire of His heart might be gratified. Tomorrow they are to be conquerors, but now He must first conquer them. The light is burning and flaming within their redeemed spirits, but the world does not see it. The purging; the purifying; the preparation within them are parts of the development of His divine purpose and plan that He Himself shall be glorified in and through His saints. Who shall reign as kings and priests unto God.

OUR GAIN

Our gain is to be indwelt by Christ! Overcome by Christ! And an overcomer is one who has first been overcome! A lullaby is much easier to listen to than God's disciplinary measures and instructions to His sons, but as a knife must needs be used to pierce the carbuncle, even so the Word of the Lord which is sharper than a two-edged sword must drain away our dross, so that we can be exercised thereby. "For no chastening for the present seemeth to be joyous but grievous; nevertheless afterward it yieldeth the peaceable fruit of righteousness unto them which are exercised thereby." (Heb. 12:11) Beloved, we are in this EXERCISE! Battle not against it! Fight not in spirit nor in body the purposes of the Lord which are being wrought out in you. We were born with a nature in which doing wrong and having our own way is as natural as breathing the air is necessary for the maintenance of our physical life! That must go! We must yield that natural propensity, that so-called reasonable desire, to the Divine Will and yield ourselves completely to the rulership of the Spirit of Life in Christ Jesus. That Life—His Resurrection Life—is the only power that can overcome the Law of sin and of death which is in operation in all of our members. We cannot be victorious unless He first is victorious in us!

We heard sometime ago of a young girl who wanted to go on the open road of evangelism because, "Granny was getting hard to live with at home!" Now, all of us have a "Granny!" Granny is not, necessarily, a call to run away! Our Father knows where the proper Granny is that will bring the boil to a head in us, that it might be pierced and bring forth healing for body, soul and spirit! Instead of running away from our individual "Granny" we should rather thank the Lord for her, because this particular "thorn in the flesh" may be ministering to our spiritual development. The victory is not in running away but in staying right where He places us, and by His grace, die to it that He may come and live in us victoriously over such circumstances. That is VICTORY! That is LIBERATION! The law of sin and death is not overcoming us, but the glorious outflow of the Resurrection Life is making us free from the law of sin and death!

We may have been mistaken in blaming everything that happens to us that we do not like on the "devil." We pick the good and praise the Lord for it and then, pitifully, moan because something comes to us that we do not want! Our Father knows that we need it and He sends us the so-called evil, but in reality, it is good, because it is for our good. Whom the Lord loveth, He chasteneth!

THE GLORY OF GOD

The Scriptures record that as Jesus passed by, He once saw a man which was blind from birth. The disciples asked Him saying, "Master who did sin, this man or his parents that he was born blind?" The reply of Jesus was that neither had sinned but "that the works of God should be made manifest in him."

Joseph said to his brethren when at last he faced them in Egypt and saw the terror on their faces when they remembered what they had done, "Ye meant it for evil, but God meant it for good." The children of Israel murmured when the Red Sea rose in front of them, and behind them they could hear the rumbling of the chariot wheels of Pharoah's army! What a time of testing it was! But how gloriously God utilized it as a type of His delivering power which shall be told through time and all eternity!

One of the most blessed moments in the life of the prophet Isaiah was when he cried, "Woe is me!" What He thought was "Woe" turned out to be victory! He saw himself as he really was and then, having seen himself in the light of his Adamic nature, he also SAW THE LORD! When he saw God, Isaiah died! "Woe is me" was the cry that left his lips, but from his death there came the life of his glorious Lord!

"The meek shall inherit the earth" because they have been made meek by surrendering to the will and purposes of God! What riches we find in the experience, "For me to live is Christ!" There is Divine Health; there is gain for body, soul and spirit. There we feel the flow of the Divine Life permeating every part of our natures until its warm, healing touch infuses the physical body and infirmities are unable to stay in the light of that Divine Presence! In days of old, when Jesus walked upon the scene, devils trembled! They begged Him to let them alone! Darkness could not withstand the light. Evil cringed before Holiness and Error fled in the revelation of the Truth which He was! Why should we not yield, willingly and obediently, to everything He has for us, whether we grasp the full significance of it at the time or not. That is the love that BELIEVETH ALL THINGS, endureth all things! It is not contending for "our rights." We have no rights but to be brought into death. We lost all our rights in the Adamic fall, but now He gives the privilege of being made alive in Him! We relinquish our authority in Adam and enter through the doorway of His sacrificial death into the Resurrection Life of the Second Adam! Then it becomes not our authority but HIS! Not our purposes but HIS! Not our plans but HIS! No longer our life but HIS! And the flow of that life brings health and strength to spirit, soul and body.

VICTORIOUS FAITH

We find in such a state of obedience that we can *laugh* at our sickness and troubles! It is there that we find that THEY ARE NOT! The imparted faith of our blessed Lord—the faith which springs up from His lovely presence within—laughs at impossibilities and crys, *"It shall be done!"* The surge of His glorious life pulsates like the ebb and flow of a mighty ocean, until we raise the victor's cry of victory! You know that you have sold out to Him! You belong to God! You want Him to run your life —your business life—your social life, until these very mortal bodies become the actual temples of the Living God! What a responsibility is lifted from your shoulders! The strain of the effort is gone! You have entered into His Rest! As you have turned the government over to Him, so the responsibility is HIS too! And He never fails. The Spirit of Him who raised up Jesus from the dead QUICKENS YOUR MORTAL BODY and you become strengthened by His Spirit in the inner man. He led you into death and, behold, you discovered it to be LIFE! He asked you to go into the tomb, and there you broke forth to the glorious consciousness of His Resurrection! There is more joy in such a walk than in having our own way! This walk of training and obedience brings us into the full condition of sons. The overcomers will sit with Him in His Throne. "To him that overcometh will I grant to sit with Me in My Throne even as I also overcame and am set down with My Father in His Throne!" (Rev. 3:21)

So we must not grumble! Rather, we must YIELD! If we are sons then we must be OBEDIENT! The whole creation, delivered from suffering and death, has been kept for the sons of God! "For I reckon that the sufferings of this present time are not worthy to be compared with the glory which shall be revealed in us; for the earnest expectation of the creature waiteth for the manifestation of the sons of God." (Rom. 8:18, 19) Hasten the day, Lord, but through Thy grace, complete the victory in us, that we may share in Thy victory when angels and men at last shall crown Thee Lord of all!

CHAPTER XII

STRENGTH IN WEAKNESS

*"And He said unto me, MY
GRACE IS SUFFICIENT
FOR THEE: FOR MY
STRENGTH IS MADE
PERFECT IN WEAKNESS.
Most gladly therefore will I
rather glory in my infirmi-
ties, that the power of
Christ may rest upon me . . .
FOR WHEN I AM WEAK
THEN AM I STRONG!"*
(II Corinthians 12:9, 10)

OFTTIMES the most precious children of the
Lord feel they know the least about the things
of God. How willing and anxious they are to do the
things that please the Father, and they say in their
hearts, "If I only knew . . ." They wait tenderly and
patiently for the knowledge of what He would have
them to do and, with all their hearts they mean it
when they say, "Have Thine own way, Lord, with
me!"

One feels the preciousness of their love of God
and their willingness to do His will but their seeming
weakness in the knowledge of the things of God, tem-

[157]

porarily, impedes their entrance into the fullness of
their inheritance. What seeming defeat they suffer in
not knowing Him, Whose they are and Whom they
long to serve!

We are reminded of a scene that occurred two
thousand years ago, upon the hill of Golgotha, when
it seemed that the strength and the love of God that
surrounded the Prince of Glory had failed! It was
a moment that seemed to portray His weakness as
He hung upon Calvary's Cross. With what seeming
defeat and shame He hung upon the Tree! We heard
the Scribes and Pharisees say, "He saved others; Himself He CANNOT save." Yes, what weakness was
apparent as the King of Glory, the One who had utterly surrendered to the will of the Father, became
OBEDIENT UNTO DEATH! He who knew no
sin became sin for each one of us. As He was hanging there in His apparent weakness, it was that He
might bring strength to those of us who find ourselves in just such weakness.

Today the cry has changed. When He hung upon
the Tree, it was "He saved others; Himself He cannot
save," but now we hear, "He saved Himself; but He
cannot save others." They deny His sufficiency for
our weakness, not knowing that His ear is open to
the faintest of our cries. They crucified Him! They
placed Him in the tomb! They thought they had
proved His weakness when they pierced His body on
Calvary, and they thought it was finished when they

laid Him in the grave. But the grave could not hold
its prey!

> *Up from the grave He arose,*
> *With a mighty triumph o'er His foes;*
> *He arose a victor o'er the dark domain,*
> *And He lives forever with His saints to reign.*
> *Hallelujah! Christ arose!*

Yes, He does live forever WITH HIS SAINTS, to
reign! We are seeing the reign of Christ in the Body
of His believers, not alone in those that know all
about Him, but in those also that love Him and are
trusting Him in spite of their weakness. His strength
is made perfect in weakness. When we are weak,
then we are STRONG, IN THE POWER OF HIS
MIGHT! Up from the grave He came and WITH
HIM CAME ALL THE REDEEMED. Salvation's
price was paid! Those who are privileged to know
some of the secrets of God, and those as well who beat
their breasts and cry, like the publican, "Have mercy
upon me, a sinner!" "For God so loved the world that
He gave His only begotten Son that whosoever believeth on Him should not perish but have everlasting life." (John 3:16)

Yes, WHOSOEVER believeth in Him shall not
fall in defeat in their own weakness, but will become
participants in that Life which was purchased
through that weakness. Strength was provided for
you and me by Him whose right it was to be strong

and powerful, but whose surrender made it possible
for Him to take our weaknesses that through His
poverty we might become rich. He is sufficient for
all His children!

LIFE FOR A LOOK

Thank God, THERE IS LIFE FOR A LOOK!
Life for a look at the Crucified One! Strength for
our weakness. Deliverance from the power of the
enemy! Strength of God enough for us all! In the
stillness of the long, night hours, when one is con-
fined on a bed of pain, it is possible TO DRINK IN
THAT STRENGTH, and not only be comforted
by the Presence of Him Whom we love, but to
BREATHE IN GOD, that we might not only be
partakers of His Divine Nature, but PARTAKERS
OF THAT STRENGTH that the world did not see
when it looked on His visible weakness on Calvary.
They did not know that out of death would spring
ETERNAL LIFE! They saw the things that "seemed
to be" and not the things that really WERE. "While
we look not at the things which are seen, but at the
THINGS WHICH ARE NOT SEEN, for the things
which are seen are temporal, but the things which
are not seen are ETERNAL!" (II Cor. 4:18)

He is our ETERNAL GOD! He is the DELIV-
ERER! It was because He knew our frame and remembered that we were dust that He came to pour
His strength into our weakness and take us by the
hand and lift us when we could never lift ourselves.

"We shall not all sleep, but we shall all be changed, in a moment, in the twinkling of an eye, at the last trump; for the trumpet shall sound, and the dead shall be raised incorruptible, and we shall be changed." (I Cor. 15:51, 52) That will be the hour of the fullness of His Triumph. That will be the day of the revelation of His strength. They called it WEAKNESS then, when He was hanging upon the accursed Tree, but that which was sown in weakness shall be raised in power by the Father's will! Caught up to meet Him in the air! Yes, from the flesh-life of weakness; from the creation that was created FROM THE DUST, He would have us share in His Triumph and become PARTAKERS OF HIS GLORY! We shall be caught up to meet Him in the air! For this, it pleased the Father to bruise Him. It was out of the bruising that HEALING came! It was out of the seeming weakness that STRENGTH was made manifest.

As we look to the Father, as we pass through the bruised experiences of our lives, we have that confidence that the Almighty God, who watcheth over Israel, neither slumbers nor sleeps! We know that HE IS TOUCHED with the feeling of our infirmities! His ear is attuned to the faintest cry. We may be lying there in seeming defeat and in apparent weakness, but it is out of such defeat that victory comes and out of such weakness that the strength of our Saviour is made manifest.

HE AROSE

The time was when He was in a grave! Low in the grave HE lay! Jesus, my Saviour! The Prince of Glory—the One whose Word had spoken the worlds into existence, and by Whose authority all things were made that are, was in apparent weakness and defeat in the cold confines of the tomb! But, Oh, how triumphantly He arose! With what victory He came forth! We, too, have this blessed Hope that as we lay in our helplessness, we have that confidence and assurance that He Who was mindful of His only begotten Son will also be mindful of *us*. We have the confidence that He Who, while permitting His Son to go to Calvary, was loving Him all of the time, in His boundless love and mercy, still remembers *us*.

God permitted His Son who, with the Father in Glory, was rich, to lay down His riches and become willing to bear our poverty and assume our sicknesses! And BY HIS STRIPES, GOD HAS PRONOUNCED US HEALED! That was the price He paid. He became partaker of our sufferings that we might become partakers of HIS STRENGTH! We see now why it was that it pleased the Father to bruise Him. It pleased the Father that through that willingness of the Son to pay the full price of our complete redemption, we might become joint-heirs to all the fullness of the Godhead! Wonderful Saviour! Matchless grace!

It was revealed to Paul that His strength would

be made perfect in our weakness. That is why he declared that the trials and testings were working out for him—and for us—a far more exceeding and eternal weight of glory! Without our need there never could be the manifestation of His abundant supply! It takes our weakness to bring forth the beauty of His strength. Peter declared, "Wherein ye greatly rejoice, though now for a season, if need be, ye are in heaviness through manifold temptations, that the trial of your faith, being much more precious than of gold that perisheth, though it be tried with fire, might be found unto praise and honour and glory at the appearing of Jesus Christ." (I Ps. 1:6, 7)

Paul saw what a privilege it was to acknowledge the Lord in all his ways. It was through such acknowledgment that Christ would fulfill the promise to that precept, and DIRECT HIS WAYS! Has the way seemed hard, my brother? Has the burden seemed heavy? Forget not that all His paths are peace, and, though for a season we see only weakness, God would have us LOOK UP and see that through the weakness of His only begotten Son, our strength was made perfect. Perfect through the strength of God, Who bore our weaknesses! The broken reed He will not break and the smoking flax He will not quench. He will be sufficient. More than sufficient, for every need of life.

He would liberate us from the bondage of this tabernacle of clay and He calls for us in the lowest place in which we find ourselves. Perhaps from our sick beds. Perhaps from our loneliness. Perhaps we have suffered betrayal at the hands of friends, and we are without the necessary means of bringing comfort. Perhaps, we have had a struggle to get the necessities of life. But in all of it, and through all of it, He is calling to us. No matter in what lowly place we find ourselves, our dungeon can FLAME WITH LIGHT! And the same glorious experience that our Saviour knew when the grave could not hold its prey can be our experience too. Our dungeon can flame with light, and we can spring up by the same Spirit's power to liberate us and make us ONE WITH HIM-SELF in that glorious ascension to the Father! But such Resurrection is not in us. It is in Him!

MADE NIGH

As He is so are we in this present age! He returned to the Father's House and He is now seated at the right hand of God, making intercession for you and for me. He prays for us. He reminds the Father of our needs and, faith whispers that the eye which watcheth over Israel neither slumbers nor sleeps. Do you, my friend, feel that He is sometimes afar off? He is made nigh, by the BLOOD! His life that was in His Blood was given for your life. Through the liberty we enjoy through the Sacrifice on Calvary, He is made nigh to us. He is not far away. He is very near! He is closer than breathing. He would minister to you of His presence and of Himself. One does not have to struggle for healing when the Healer is so very near!

Have you ever whispered the word, "JESUS" and let it drop again and again from the depths of your heart? "Jesus, have mercy upon me!" Say it until you can say it with such worshipful tones that you can feel the course of His life flowing and pulsating through your being. Say it in faith that He hears and that it pleases Him that you are calling. Yes, He is the Friend, willing to be called in the day of trouble and He has promised TO DELIVER! We are not asking Him for something that He gives, but we are waiting for the MANIFESTATION OF HIMSELF! And He gives Himself so freely! His ear is open to the faintest of our cries and His heart is touched with the feeling of our infirmities. "He that spared not His own Son, but delivered Him up for us all, how shall He not with Him also freely give us ALL THINGS!" (Rom. 8:32) All things! Nothing does He withhold for He Who possesses all things, freely and gladly gives us Himself.

His strength has been made perfect and that perfect strength is such that in all of our weaknesses, it can be made manifest! It leaves nothing out. It suffices for every need of the body and soul and spirit. He has promised to supply all our need. Just what is YOUR need? Whatever it be, you can draw nigh with full assurance that as we call to Him, His answer

is on the way. There is a balm in Gilead. There is
DELIVERANCE FOR THE CAPTIVE! There is
healing for the sick because that which was sown in
weakness was raised in might and in power! Christ
is SUFFICIENT! He is all we need!

THE LORD ANSWERS

How often when we find ourselves in a weakened
condition do we feel the nearness of our Father. In
the days of our seeming strength, when no difficulties
or troubles assail us, the heart will sometimes become
stony and we do not feel our need of God. But when
our weakness is made apparent, it changes our stony
heart, because we find that we are insufficient in ourselves to change circumstances and conditions. We
are helpless in our weakness! We acknowledge our
insufficiency before the Lord. Then the Deliverer
comes! "This poor man cried unto the Lord and He
delivered him out of all of his troubles." Yes "this
poor man cried." There was nothing else he could
do. He needed help and he knew from whence that
help would come. I presume that this poor man knew
little of the deep things of God, but that would not
exclude the Heavenly Father from hearing him. Men
do not approach the Father because of their knowledge of Him, but they come through Him who is
the DOOR, and there is no other way to the Father's
presence but the way of the Saviour. So this poor
man cried! I have cried many times to God. Have

you? I have cried for His presence and for His wisdom that was so needed, but He has never failed me, and I am sure He will never fail you. *His strength is made perfect through our weakness.* We need not condemn ourselves; neither must we condemn each other, for ofttimes our weakness is a road that leads near the heart of God.

Somehow, we walk on "tiptoes" when there is apparent weakness. It is often at the time of weakness that we take the "shoes from off our feet" for it is then that we feel the nearness of the Lord. At the approach of the Eternal, the noise of human feet would seem irreverent. He calls, "BE STILL AND KNOW THAT I AM GOD." It is when we need Him that He comes. It is to meet our emptiness that He comes with His fullness. How many times have I been conscious of His lovely presence suddenly appearing in the sickroom, coming with His grace and love and strength to meet the helplessness of one of the weakest of His children. "Be still and know that I am God!" Not only be still in the noise which our humanity would make, but BE STILL WITHIN. Be still, knowing that GOD IS, and that He is a Rewarder of them that diligently seek Him. We can draw nigh with full assurance that He, which hath begun will PERFECT the work! He will not fail! It was in the day when Abraham's faith was slipping and the ground was trembling beneath his feet and he had come to a place of His own weakness that the

Lord cried this message of strength into the ears of this failing man. "I am EL SHADDAI!" He was the GOD WHO WAS ENOUGH. He was then and HE IS NOW! Always sufficient and as He did to His servant of old, He can do the same for us today. As He pours out freely His love and life and strength, we can hear Him sweetly say, "Walk before me and be thou perfect!" Wonderful EL SHADDAI!

HOW OFTEN WOULD I

With each succeeding day in the affairs of this world, we are made to know the apparent weakness of those who have been called to rule the nations. We hear them crying "Peace, Peace" when there is no peace and the passing hours find them deeper in a maze of complications from which there seems to be no escape. They have failed to recognize the extended ARM OF THE LORD! They have refused to take God into account! This is true not only of the individual man in his weakness, but of the nation whose manifest weakness is now seen by the whole world. In the days of old, Jesus stood beneath the trees of Bethphage and cried, "O, Jerusalem, Jerusalem, how often would I have gathered thee under the wings of My protecting care and love, as a mother hen gathereth her brood, but ye would not." That was the message of Christ. HOW OFTEN WOULD I, but *ye* would not! He was not only speaking to the individual then, for in those arms of love and healing,

He would have embraced the whole city. How willing He is. How enduring His love and patience.

God is not willing that any should perish but that all should come to repentance. That means ALL of us; no matter in what situation we find ourselves and no matter how complex the complications of life may be. We should not become discouraged if we find that we have made alliances with those who believe not God. We often find our lives so entangled in business associations and, sometimes, domestic relationships, that we conclude that it is impossible for us to serve the Lord. How far from the truth that is! WITH GOD ALL THINGS ARE POSSIBLE. He will not fail us. The greater the need, the greater His grace. The more apparent our weakness and the more we acknowledge it, the more will be the manifestation of His strength. We have known some lives that have become so entangled with the affairs of this world and the associations with unbelievers that one would have thought that they never could be delivered. But they began to DEAL WITH GOD! The heart opened to Him, and they found that they were dealing with the GREAT DELIVERER!

HE WILL NOT FAIL

There must first be a WILLING HEART, on our part, and from that willingness and our confessed weakness, the Spirit of God will be begin to work. It is not always as rapidly as we desire, but when we have an EYE SINGLE and a heart open to Him, little by little the clouds roll away and, eventually, they become dissipated. Each passing day will find us more conscious of God and we shall become so encouraged as we take inventory of all that He has done that we will be assured of what He will do on our behalf. He will not begin the work without completing it. He will always lead us in a very plain path. We must learn to leave it completely in His care and entrust ourselves to the guidance of His hand and His keeping power.

If we become anxious and think we can take the affairs of our lives in our own hands, we may MAR His pattern. We may try to hasten our deliverance but we must remember that it has taken many years of disobedience to the will of God for such entanglements to come. God has been patient with us in *our* will and *our* way for so many years. Can we not, in patience, possess our souls, as He begins to extricate us from the webs of our own disobedience? He will never condemn us for what we have done in the past; but with God each day is a FRESH BEGINNING. Each day brings NEW HOPE; each passing hour new assurance! My son, give Me thine heart! And from that point, on, the pilgrimage Home is started. Each day our burdens become lighter and each day He seems to assume the greater part of the load until we find, in that fellowship that there has been a vertable EXCHANGE OF LIVES. He has taken our burdens and left us with a song! He has given us the oil of joy for mourning and beauty for ashes. His gift has been sunshine for our shadow; His strength is made perfect in our weakness.

So do not weep, beloved, if today you find yourself in weakness. Look away to the Deliverer! If you are in bondage, the Emancipator is very nigh. Plant the seed of your weakness in the Garden of God's Love and let Him water and care for it. He will touch it and it will spring up into Resurrection Life. And the fruit from such a tree will please the Father and you will be brought, ultimately, to your desired haven! *His strength is made perfect in your weakness!*

WITH HIM

When Jesus walked on Salem's streets,
Or trod the shores of Galilee,
And caused the lame man to be whole,
The deaf to hear, the blind to see;
'Twas not alone because He was
The Son of God of virgin born,
And angels sang through riven skies
To greet Him on His natal morn;

It was His Father who endued
Him with the Father's life and power;
The strength by which He overcame
Was given for the testing hour.
He was the Son, and yet He learned
Obedience by the things He bore;
And thus He saw His Father's face
On mountain lone or lakeside shore.

The works He did; the words He spake,
Were not His own. The Father's they.
'Twas by the Father that He lived
And healed, and preached; taught us to pray
"Our Father" too; made heaven near,
And bade the seas of life be still;
Poured out His life blood freely in
Obedience to the Father's will.

He is the channel through which streams
The riches of God's grace and love.
He is the way, the truth, the life
The only Door that leads above
To realms of Spirit, where we meet
The Author of redeeming grace,
And see the glory of our God
Illuminate the Saviour's face.

But as He by the Father lived
So we His sons shall live by Him.
And He who is the light of life
Shines with a light that cannot dim;
Shines in the sons who know their God;
Who feast upon the living Word;
Whose lives become the riverbed
For flowing glories of the Lord.

With Him they died; with Him they live;
With Him from guarded tomb they rise;
They breathe the Resurrection Life;
Ascend with Him through azure skies;
And sit with Him in places high
At right hand of the Father's Throne,
And hear the Son in triumph claim
Redemption's children as His own.

Is this of works, or can we earn
Such glories by the servant's skill?
Or enter into heaven's realm
By operation of the will?
Forbid it, Lord; for us to live
Is Christ; and in His life alone
We find the Resurrection power
That lifts us to the Father's Throne.

—*Charles* S. *Price.*

CPSIA information can be obtained
at www.ICGtesting.com
Printed in the USA
BVHW041426171121
621811BV00008B/166